Hot for Words

HARPER

NEW YORK • LONDON • TORONTO • SYDNEY

Hot for

Words

Answers to All Your
Burning Questions about
Words and Their Meanings

MARINA ORLOVA

HarperCollins books may be purchased for educational, business, or sales promotional use. For information, please write: Special Markets Department, HarperCollins Publishers, 10 East 53rd Street, New York, NY 10022.

FIRST EDITION

Designed by Janet M. Evans
Photographs on pages ii, iii, iv, 159 © Jennifer Moss
All other photographs © Derek Caballero

Library of Congress Cataloging-in-Publication Data is available upon request.

ISBN 978-0-06-177631-1

09 10 11 12 13   OV/RRD   10 9 8 7 6 5 4 3

TO MY PARENTS
who encouraged me to
study philology, and

TO MY FRIEND CHARLES COMO,
whose short e-mail
"YouTube.com, check it out,"
introduced me to a whole
new way of teaching.

Your Class Schedule

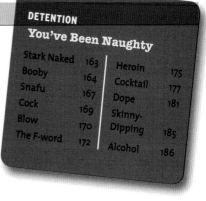

Introduction

Why do our parents use "the birds and the bees" to explain reproduction to us? And did you really have to get the King's permission before practicing what "the birds and the bees" do back in medieval England? Why was America named after a guy who didn't discover it? Oh, and what does *OK* stand for?

These are the types of questions that keep me awake at night.

When you start looking at the origins of words, it opens up a whole new world for you—a world with a great view of history—in little, bite-sized chunks.

Once you've been exposed to the amazing world of words, you will suddenly find yourself asking more and more questions about where words and phrases come from. That is the goal of this book: to get you curious about the world of word origins, and about your own society's history, as revealed through word origins.

I can assure you that once this bug bites you, you will forever be hooked, and you will find yourself looking at words in a new and different way. Who would have thought that the world of word origins could be so exciting?

OK—class is in session, so please keep the noise down in the back, and let's get started!

Homeroom

The Bare Essentials

School

> In the old days—the very old days—being able to go to "school" meant you had a lot of time on your hands.

THAT'S BECAUSE THE WORD *SCHOOL* comes from the Greek word *schole*, meaning "leisure." Greek philosophers like Aristotle and Plato used to gather groups of young men who weren't going to be distracted by mundane activities like working a job; they taught these young men, and called the gatherings "schole"— a name that carried the clear suggestion that these students could afford to spend their time doing something that most other people couldn't.

The name stuck, and later on, the Romans turned the Greek word that had come to mean "gathering of students" into *schola*, which in turn gave rise to English words like *school*, *scholastic*, and *scholar*. Nowadays, the idea that only cultured, leisured people should go to school has fallen out of favor . . . one can only wish that school time were still considered leisurely!

When you use the word *school* in the phrase "school of fish," you're using a word with the same spelling, but a different lineage. That's because the word *school* in "school of fish" descends from a Dutch word that's akin to the Old English word *scolu*, meaning "gathering of people."

TRUE OR FALSE

A *school* can also mean, "A group of persons drinking together in a bar or public house, and taking turns buying the drinks."

ANSWER True. Now, who wants to buy the first round?

I am ...

A. an etymologist
B. a philologist
C. a nicebecetur
D. all of the above

(Answer: d. A nicebecetur is a fine, dainty, or fashionable woman. Some people will try to tell you that the word is obsolete, but I just used it, which makes this book a published, contemporary citation of modern usage. Draw your own conclusion.)

Etymology

THE WORD *ETYMOLOGY* itself has an etymology, an origin. The first half comes from the Greek word *etymos,* which means "true," and the second half comes from the Greek word for "word," which is *logos*. An etymologist, then, is someone who finds out the truth about words, someone who separates myth from history in the field of language.

This is a fascinating job to have, because there are stories inside every word, just as there are stories inside every person, every community, and every country. Of course, not all of the stories we hear about words are true; some are false, and some are just plain bizarre. In this book, you and I will get to the bottom of some of the best stories.

Philology

I confess: I am in love with the English language. And no entry in this book serves as better evidence of the kind of long-running, public love affair I have chosen to pursue than *philology*—a word that proves once and for all that my life's work really is (in the immortal words of Tina Turner) a "love thing."

PHILOLOGY TRACES ITS ANCESTRY through an old Latin word, *philologia*, that literally means "love of learning" or "love of letters." That Latin word came from two Greek words, *philo* (meaning "love") and *logos*, (meaning "word" or "speech"). To me, *philology* will always mean the love of words.

Now I want you to visualize a rushing river that is barreling through time and space, from Ancient Greece toward the twenty-first century, carrying you and me along with it. Up ahead, the river is about to split off into three different directions. In modern English, the river we are riding, the river called *philology*, has divided into different fast-running, complementary streams of meaning. One branch of the river is the study of the relationship of languages, and especially the study of the history of languages as reflected in their texts; a second branch of the river means *just* the study of old texts to learn more about a people or a culture; and a third branch means *just* the study of literature. (Yet another branch, meaning "the science of language itself," has never really caught on in the United States, and is likely to flow instead into conversations of linguistics, as we shall see in the next entry.)

Which branch of the river will we take? I say we take all three . . . wherever they lead.

The field of "comparative philology" identified unexpected similarities between Sanskrit and European languages—and postulated a hypothetical common language that lay behind both sets of language traditions.

ANSWER True. The hypothetical common language is known today as Proto-Indo-European.)

Linguistics

What does language do?

This seems like an easy question at first, but if you stop to think about it, you'll realize it's more complicated than it seems.

HERE'S MY ANSWER: Language *describes* the world for us, but it also *shapes our world* as we describe it—either to ourselves or someone else.

As it happens, the linguist Benjamin Lee Whorf, author of *Language, Thought, and Reality,* agrees with me on this one. He wrote, "Language shapes the way we think, and determines what we can think about." Whorf also believed that we human beings "dissect nature along lines laid down by our native language. Language is not simply a reporting device for experience, but a defining framework for it."

The word *linguistics* itself, which broadly means "that which pertains to language or languages," can show us how words can both inform us and shape our world in the process. For instance: If I were to tell you that you should learn more about linguistics, you might decide to ignore me. Yet if I were to tell you that *linguist* derives from the Latin *lingua,* meaning "language" or "tongue" . . . and if I were to add that the way we use *linguistics* today draws on a much older meaning—"one who uses his tongue freely"—perhaps you would be interested in looking a little more deeply at linguistics. Suddenly, it's possible that you would be motivated to find out what this linguistics business is all about! Language has just shaped your experience (and mine as well) by appealing to the unique inner resonances of a word, in this case, the word *tongue*.

These resonances are what determine our reality.

Linguistics is the response to the impulse within the human mind that asks: How do languages vary? How do human beings acquire language, anyway? What role does language itself play in determining human experience? And what exactly did she mean by "using one's tongue freely"?

Linguists are a rare and predominantly nerdy breed, but they maintain an abiding authority in my world because of their ability to shed light on subjects like phonetics (the study of the physical properties of speech), phonology (the study of sounds), morphology (the study of the internal structure of words), syntax (the study of how humans create meaning in grammatical sentences), and semantics (the study of how meaning itself is created by means of words, phrases, and sentences).

All of this, initially, might sound very deep . . . but I hope to show you in this book that it can all be quite a lot of fun.

 In addition to being a linguist, Noam Chomsky is . . .

a. a philosopher
b. a cognitive scientist
c. a controversial political activist
d. one of the most-cited living scholars
e. all of the above

(Answer: e. And did you know that a chimpanzee who was the subject of an animal language acquisition study was named Nim Chimpsky as a pun on Chomsky's name?)

Eponym

An eponym is simply a word named after a real or imagined personality. The word comes from the Greek *epi-*, meaning "upon," and *onyma*, meaning "name." Some eponyms are obvious: *Aphrodisiac*, for instance, is named after the Greek goddess of love, Aphrodite. Some are less so: The word *maverick* is named after a politician, Samuel Augustus Maverick, who refused to brand his cattle. People would point to unbranded cattle roaming around and say, "Oh, that's Maverick's"—meaning his cattle.

MOST EPONYMS have fascinating stories behind them, and I will share some of my favorites with you in this book. You'll find words like *Adam's apple, Amazon, America, blurb, boycott, chauvinist, eggs Benedict, gerrymander, philander, siren, tantalize,* and *vandal.* Some words and phrases sound like they ought to be eponyms, but really aren't. They're covered in this book as well. (For example, *hooker*, p. 41; "His name is mud," p. 102; and Uncle Sam, p. 147.)

The practice of creating an eponym is known as *eponymy.*

One of the earliest known examples of eponomy occurred when ...

A. the ancient Assyrians named a year after a political figure

B. the Romans named a year after the two consuls who served during that year

C. a royal European family adopted a system of regnal dating that numbered years by the sequence in which they occurred in the living monarch's tenure

D. Donald Trump named approximately half of Manhattan after himself

(Answer: a. The person after whom the years were named was called the "limmu." In the period of history known as Old Assyrian [twentieth to sixteenth centuries BC], reigning monarchs could not have the year named after them; the year's namesake was typically some appointed royal official. In later periods, however, the kings started taking this honor for themselves.)

Mathematics

As we all know, intelligence is sexy—and intelligence about mathematics is particularly sexy. Why? Because the most ancient root for this word connects to the concepts of both thinking and arousal. If you've ever found yourself stimulated by square roots, or anything else having to do with figures, read on.

TO UNDERSTAND THE CONNECTION between the word *mathematics* and arousal, you've got to go back to this word's oldest known root, which is from a language even more ancient than ancient Greek. This language is known today as Proto-Indo-European, but with no written evidence, we have no idea what it was called at the time. In fact, we're not absolutely certain what form this hypothetical language took. But it seems to have passed on root words to lots of different language systems. Everything we know about it is based on its influence on other languages, including Greek. One of these influential root words is *men* or *mon*—which means "to think, or to have one's mind aroused." From this root, the Greeks appear to have created the word *mathema*, meaning "science, knowledge, or mathematical studies." (The same root is also at the heart of the words *mind* and *mental*.)

Today, when Americans are in a hurry and don't have time for a four-syllable word, they condense *mathematics* to a singular short form, *math*, while the British hold on to the plural form, *maths*. Maths was used first, because it described a number of mathematical disciplines, including geometry, astronomy, and optics. On the one hand, the British are

Which of the following people did not win a Nobel Prize in mathematics?

A. yours truly
B. Albert Einstein
C. Niels Bohr
D. Steve Jobs
E. all of the above

(Answer: e. There is no Nobel Prize in mathematics.)

probably technically right, because you certainly wouldn't say you were taking a class in "mathematic." Then again, should we really be taking language advice from people who drive lorries instead of trucks? And on the wrong side of the road, no less? When it comes to adding an extra *s* to *math*, you're on your own.

Literature

FROM THE LATIN *LITERA,* which means "letter." A writer who has accomplished great things in poetry, drama, fiction, or memoir is sometimes called a "man (or woman) of letters." This doesn't mean that the person's handwriting is remarkably neat, of course; it means that the content of the person's written work is considered inspiring. So, writing that really matters is known as *literature.* What's interesting is that *literature* is also applied to more trivial "letters" like tracts, pamphlets, and sales brochures—as in, "I'm going to send you some literature about our company."

From the same Latin root, we get the English words *literal, literate, illiterate,* and, of course, *letter,* all of which connect directly or indirectly to concepts of reading or writing. We also get the word *literati,* who are men of letters, which gave us the suffix *-erati,* which was then used to make such words as *glitterati* ("glittering" stars of the fashionable or literary world), *digerati* (computer experts), and *blogerati*—you can guess that one! What's next? *SMSerati? Twitterati?*

Letters Home is a collection of the once-private letters of . . .

A. Bill Clinton
B. Sylvia Plath
C. Donald Trump
D. William Wordsworth
E. Princess Diana

(Answer: b. The collection was published posthumously in 1975.)

P.E.

Let's Get Physical

Who was the buxom blonde who starred in the 1953 movie *Gentlemen Prefer Blondes*?

A.   Marilyn Monroe
B.   Pamela Anderson
C.   Veronica Lake
D.   Jane Russell

(Answer: a)

Buxom

THIS ORIGINALLY MEANT "flexible" or "pliant"—it came from the word *bugan*, meaning "to bend." It was a compliment in the old days: someone who was "buxom" was adaptable, kind, and submissive. People talked about being "buxom" to authority figures like the pope, and what they meant was being obedient.

From there, *buxom* went on a long, strange trip. For a while, "obedient" maintained its living quarters inside this word's meaning, but was accompanied by a roommate: "cheerfully carefree." The connection here was possibly that people who were obedient were thought to live simpler, happier lives. Eventually, though, "obedient" moved out and found other living arrangements.

In the period following the twelfth century, other residents of *buxom* included "healthy" and "vigorous." That meaning was eventually replaced by a new occupant, "pleasantly plump," which came along in the late 1500s. Today, the word serves as a wink-and-a-nod synonym for "full-figured" (I think you know what that means) and can also just mean "full-bosomed," which is oftentimes the most visible part of a full-figured woman! Politically correct dictionaries describe this usage as "dated," but I see it all the time, so I'm not sure how dated it really is. Perhaps the dictionaries mean to say the use of this word is a little dangerous in certain settings, like the workplace. You probably wouldn't want to describe the CEO of your company as "buxom" during a staff meeting, even if she is.

Interestingly, the word is often combined with *blonde*, and rarely with *brunette*. I'm not sure how the brunettes feel about that, but personally, I'm grateful for this emphasis in usage. Can you think of a particular buxom blonde right now? Try.

The word *mouse*, which shares a common lineage with the word *muscle*, is now used to describe the tool that moves a computer cursor around. This usage of mouse dates back to ...

A.   1965
B.   1975
C.   1985
D.   1996

(Answer: a)

Muscle

Why is a *muscle* called a *muscle*? I started worrying about this after researching the word *bimbo,* which is "an attractive woman seemingly without intellectual capacity." One of my dear students contacted me to bring me up to date on the new word *gymbo,* which one has to see spelled out to understand. This is the male equivalent of a *bimbo*—a male of limited mental capacity who spends all of his available time at the gym. (Another variation is *himbo,* a non-gym-obsessed male bimbo.) This led me to a discussion of the difference between a *goon* and a *geek.* They're both guys, of course—one has brawn, but very little brains, and the other has brains, but very little brawn. And that left me thinking about the word *muscle.*

IT TURNS OUT that *muscle* comes from the French word *musculus,* which in turn comes from the Latin *musculus,* meaning "mouse."

"Mouse"?

Yes, "mouse." Lift up your sleeve and expose your bicep. Now flex your muscle. Watch your bicep closely. It kind of looks like something is moving around, doesn't it? It almost looks like a little mouse running around there under your skin. Right?

Well, somebody thought it did. That's why the Latin word for "mouse" came into play. Keep that in mind the next time you run into a goon who calls you a "geek" and asks you whether you're a "man" or a "mouse."

Now I want you to think of other body parts named after animals. E-mail them to me, as I'd be interested to see what you come up with. You can send them to: bodyparts@hotforwords.com.

Adam's Apple

THE NAME ADAM comes from the Hebrew word for "man," *adam*, which literally means "one formed from the ground," as that word comes from the Hebrew word *adamah*, which means "ground." In other words, the etymology of this name tells us that the biblical Adam was literally formed by God from earth, soil, or, in some of the more interesting accounts, clay. Etymologists think the modern phrase *Adam's apple* may descend from a mistranslation of the Hebrew phrase *tappuah haadam*, which means "a man's swelling."

Yes, I said "a man's swelling." Stop giggling in the back there, please.

Haadam means "the man" and *tappuah* means "a swelling," but the Hebrew word for apple sounds similar to *tappuah*, hence the possible mistranslation. Let me explain why.

The formal medical name for the Adam's apple is . . .

A. laryngeal prominence
B. sin originalis
C. throatus lumpus
D. glandula thyroidea
E. the Adam's apple

(Answer: a)

In the book of Genesis, we're told that Eve gave Adam a piece of forbidden fruit, which he ate (the Bible doesn't say anything about it being an apple). The phrase *Adam's apple* seems to have arisen as an attempt to make sense of *tappuah haddam,* and explain that lumpy, "swollen" portion of the human throat that men have and women don't.

So now you have an explanation of *that* male lump. It's a piece of the ancient forbidden fruit that has lodged permanently in the throats of the sons of Adam—a timeless reminder, perhaps, of male susceptibility to female provocation.

Nude gymnasts . . .

A. do not really exist
B. won laurels of victory in ancient Greece
C. won three gold medals in the 1948
   Helsinki Olympic Games
D. were given special compensation in
   ancient Greece if they painted the logos
   of certain Greek merchants prominently
   on their bodies

(Answer: b)

Gymnastics

> Did you know that the ancient Greek athletes used to train and compete in the nude? It's true!

THE WORD GYMNASTICS COMES FROM the Greek word *gymnos*, which means "nude." Greek athletes—only the male ones—would strip to their birthday suits when the time came to compete for high honors in Olympic competitions. Not surprisingly, the games were very popular. They would have been even more popular, I think, if the women had been allowed to train and compete in similarly nonexistent attire. (Maybe the organizing officials were concerned about the athletes—or the spectators—getting distracted.) Many Greeks of that time believed that going about naked was good for the health, including the great physician Hippocrates.

Unfortunately, the spectators didn't get to enjoy all the benefits of wandering around in the buff—just the athletes.

Nudity in the Olympics, sadly, was banned in A.D. 393 by Emperor Theodosius I, due to its pagan influences. By the time the Olympics were relaunched in 1896 in Athens, Greece, the nude-athlete thing had been long forgotten, thanks to the long-standing influence of both the Romans and Christianity, which embraced a medieval conception of the human body as base and sinful. Supposedly, we're past all that now, but I haven't heard anyone advocating an all-nude modern Olympics. I suppose the television ratings would be very impressive—though the Winter Olympics might be rather tough, wouldn't you agree?

"Head over Heels"

When we say someone fell "head over heels," we mean the person took a serious tumble, right? Stop and think for a moment, though. Isn't your head *already* above your heels, even before you start to fall? If you picture someone in the act of falling really badly, like down a flight of stairs, do you picture the person's head being higher, or lower, than the person's heels?

Wouldn't it make more sense to say, "heels over head"?

ACTUALLY, IT *WOULD* MAKE MORE SENSE to say that—and it *did* make more sense to say that for hundreds of years. The original Middle English expression was "heels over head," but for some reason people switched it around, probably because they liked the sound of "head over heels" better. The same thing

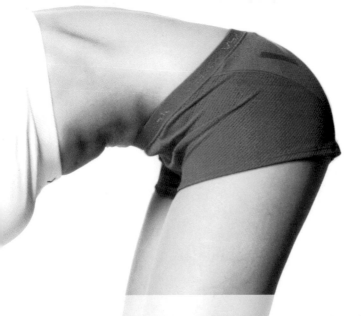

happened to the expression, "You can't have your cake and eat it, too." The original expression was "You can't eat your cake and have it," coined around 1562, as that makes sense—once you eat your cake, it will be gone, and you can't have something that is already gone, right?

The expression, "The proof is in the pudding," means . . .

A. the evidence is buried

B. the results are what count

C. you should finish what you start

(Answer: b. The original expression was, "The proof of the pudding is in the eating," meaning that "to fully test something out, you must experience it." For example, it's the taste of the pudding that counts! The word *proof* means "to test," which is not used very often these days except in such phrases as *proofread* and *proving ground*.)

Jockey

THIS COMES FROM a Scottish proper name, *Jock*, that's a variant of the common modern name *Jack*. In the early 1500s, *jock* meant "boy" or "fellow"—the equivalent of the modern *dude*. But by 1670, *jock* had taken on the meaning "one who rides horses during racing events." How? The most popular—and likely—explanation is that *jock* or its diminutive form *jockey* had become a widely popular nickname for horse dealers, and that the blurring of the line between someone who traded in horses and someone who raced them competitively took place over about a century and a half. From there, *jockey* settled in for a long ride.

In much later years, the word *jock* was appropriated as a piece of vulgar slang referring to a man's private parts—whether he rode horses or not. The protective supporting gear known as the "jock strap" derives from this usage.

The name Jack is a nickname for what name?

A. Jim
B. John
C. Jefferson
D. George

(Answer: b. Jack is a common nickname for John, which seems odd as it's the same number of letters! John F. Kennedy's nickname was "Jack.")

Sex Ed

The Naked Truth

"The Birds and the Bees"

Why is it "the birds and the bees"? Why not "the bunnies and the kitty-cats"? For one thing, it's easy to demonstrate birds laying eggs and bees pollinating flowers without embarrassing yourself too much in front of the children. What's more, there's force in numbers: "the birds and the bees" has always seemed to be the analogy everyone else was using. But why is that?

WELL, THE FIRST PRINTED EXAMPLE of the exact phrase "the birds and the bees" being used as a metaphor for human sexuality shows up in 1939, though birds and bees appeared in poetry long before then. It may have been the popular 1928 Cole Porter song, "Let's Fall in Love," which talked a lot about birds doing "it," and bees doing "it," and even educated fleas doing "it," that brought the expression to the mainstream. Personally, I never thought that falling in love was the "it" Cole Porter was really getting at there, and apparently neither did the parents. Let's face it: when it comes to falling in love, the emotional capacity of a flea, even an educated one, seems pretty limited.

Reproduction seems more likely to be the topic Porter was actually driving at, and the parents of the day used the analogy of the birds and the bees (fortunately leaving out the fleas) to educate their children—who eventually learned the lesson about the "birds and the bees" well enough to become our parents!

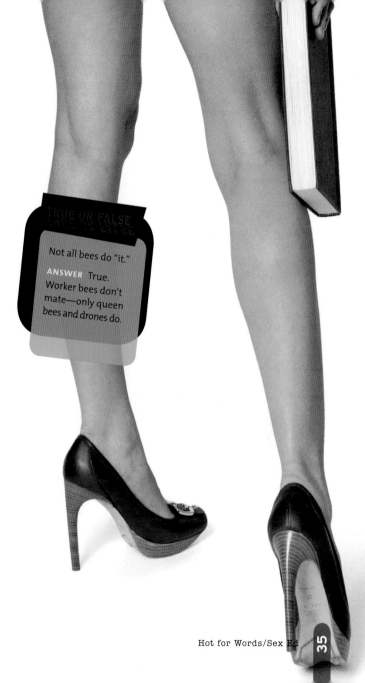

TRUE OR FALSE

Not all bees do "it."

ANSWER True.
Worker bees don't
mate—only queen
bees and drones do.

Erotic

THE ANCIENT GREEKS WORSHIPPED a lot of different gods, one of whom was called *Eros*. This god was, in the complex Greek system of deities, the fairest of them all. The problem was, Eros had an attitude. He was self-absorbed and cruel, and, just for fun, he shot deadly arrows into the hearts not just of men, but of other gods as well.

This capricious guy was, according to the Greeks, the god of love. They held a festival in his name known as the *Erotia* or *Erodita*, and during this festival, husbands and wives who had been fighting were supposed to kiss and make up. From this notion of marital reconciliation—and, presumably, makeup sex—we get the word *erotic*, which means "arousing, or tending to arouse, sexual desire."

The writer C. S. Lewis had an interesting insight on eroticism: "Eros will have naked bodies; Friendship naked personalities." I think one can be much scarier than the other. I'll leave it to you to figure out which is which.

The Romans, like the Greeks, had a god of love. Who was he?

A. Odin
B. Zeus
C. Bacchus
D. Cupid

(Answer: d. In the Roman tradition, Cupid was the symbol of passionate love who fell in love with a mortal, Psyche.)

Orgy

We come now to another one of those words that many of my dear students have been very interested in discussing. I have to assume that this is because of all the scholars out there, both professional and amateur, who have an abiding interest in ancient rites connected with another Greek god: Dionysius.

IF YOU ARE ONE OF THOSE DIONYSIUS FANS, you already know that thousands of years ago the Greeks held special festivals for this god of wine and revelry in the middle of the night. During these events, which started out with secret rituals in honor of Dionysius, the genders mixed, the dancing and singing got wild, and the sex laws were ignored. In other words, a party out of bounds.

The Greeks had a word for these get-togethers: *orgia*. That simply meant "secret rites." Back then, of course, the secret rites were an essential prerequisite of—or, let's face it, maybe just an excuse for—wild sex. These days, we use the term *orgy* to describe sexual encounters in a group setting, or to refer to any instance of unrestrained revelry or heedless overindulgence. Dionysius doesn't seem to have much of anything to do with the proceedings anymore.

If you were wondering, in a purely objective and academic manner, whether *orgasm* shares a common derivation with *orgy*, you may be interested to know that they come from two entirely different Greek words: *orgia*, meaning private or secret rites, and *organ*, meaning "to swell or become excited." That first Greek word, *orgia*, is an ancient ancestor not only of *orgy*, but of the modern verb *urge*. The second, *organ*, "to swell," is actually unrelated to the musical instrument or internal part of the body—those organs come from the Greek *organon*, which means, simply enough, a "musical instrument" or "organ of the body."

Actress Jane Fonda won an Oscar for portraying a hooker. Can you name the 1971 film?

A. *They Shoot Horses, Don't They?*

B. *Klute*

C. *Coming Home*

D. *The China Syndrome*

(Answer: b)

Hooker

SOME PEOPLE WILL TELL YOU that the word *hooker* (meaning "a prostitute") derives from the vast sea of prostitutes that followed the Army of the Potomac, which was under the command of General Joseph Hooker during the American Civil War. As a matter of history, the Army of the Potomac did know what it liked from these women, and it was willing to pay for it. There is a problem with this seemingly simple explanation of the word's origin, however: a documented usage of *hooker* to mean "prostitute" dates from about two decades before the Civil War began. It shows up in 1845 in a letter between students at the University of North Carolina: "If he comes by way of Norfolk, he will find any number of pretty hookers in the Brick Row not far from French's Hotel."

Although Hooker's hookers don't connect to the true origin of the word, they point toward a more intriguing truth: sometimes a word's meaning can solidify because of a coincidence. This is one of those times. The voracious appetites of the soldiers under the command of General Hooker probably accelerated the process by which those plying the world's oldest profession came to be known as *hookers*—even though Hooker's men did not originate the label themselves.

The connection between *prostitute* and *hooker*, which seems to have arisen sometime in the early nineteenth century, probably arose because the process of finding a new customer in this profession, as in so many others, is similar to the act of fishing: one baits a hook and waits for a nibble. Usage of *hook* in this figurative sense—though not specifically referring to prostitutes—dates back to the fifteenth century. An earlier use of *hook,* as one of the tools of a well-trained thief, who stole items through open windows with a hook, may also have played a role here.

Horny

FOR SOME STRANGE REASON, *lots* of my dear students have requested that I explain the derivation of this word. So, eager students, let's play a little game here. I'll give you three possible origins of this word. See if you can pick the correct one.

The word *horny* now describes sexual arousal because . . .

A. the Vikings had a ritual, popular circa A.D. 1000, of blowing a special horn when they wanted to have sexual intercourse. The sound of the horn meant that women had to go to the source of the sound and have sexual intercourse with the men.

B. the English Puritans believed that sexual desires were the work of the Devil, and that those who provoked and encouraged such desires might as well be wearing the devil's horns

C. a man's private part, when aroused, looks kind of like a horn

(Answer: C. The English word *horn* is quite old, dating back to the Proto-Indo-European *ker-*, which means the "uppermost part of the body." The expression "to have horn" comes from the late eighteenth century.)

Is it good or bad to be a "housewife"?

What is your opinion? Go online to
www.hotforwords.com/housewife and vote.

**In referring to a woman, which of these
words would *not* get you slapped?**

A.   tart
B.   crow
C.   shawnty
D.   hoochie

(Answer: C. A *shawnty* is a showy, smart person,
which is a combination of *genteel*, meaning "among
the gentry," and *jaunty*, meaning "well-bred.")

Hussy

Often preceded by the word *brazen* (meaning "showing or expressing boldness and complete lack of shame"), *hussy* is not used as a compliment these days, but as an insult: "an immoral woman." Or, if you prefer a little less euphemism, "a slut."

IN A FORMER INCARNATION, as *huswif,* the word was not an insult, but neutral or even positive. It simply meant a thrifty, focused, "woman of the house," or, literally, "housewife." Over the centuries, the shortened form of *huswif* came to mean a young woman engaged in such menial activities as milking cows or tending to crops, and, from this active platform, eventually came to describe a woman who was active in other areas as well, and who would boldly have sex with pretty much anyone she liked.

It's interesting what people get touchy about: nowadays, both *housewife* and *hussy* are considered off-limits when describing actual, living people. The *Encarta World English Dictionary*, for its part, lists *housewife* as "dated." The feminists of the 1970s were fond of pointing out that no one ever actually married a house, which is true; they energetically promoted the word *homemaker* in place of *housewife*. No one has yet to come up with an acceptable alternative for *hussy*, though. Encarta won't even acknowledge the word's existence, which seems a little odd for a word that has been in wide use since at least the middle of the seventeenth century. Political correctness, too, can exhibit a complete lack of shame.

Wedding

When you think of a wedding, what images first spring to mind? Some people instantly think of things like extended family, heartfelt toasts, and badly dressed live bands playing mediocre eighties music. Other people think of Las Vegas.

AS IT TURNS OUT, the people in the second group have etymology on their side, because the English word *wed* originally meant "to gamble," and it was in this sense that *wedding* came to describe matrimony. In the same way that one might gamble on a horse, one gambled—and, alas, sometimes lost—when one took marriage vows. (By the way, in the old days in England, brides and bridegrooms pledged their faith to each other "for fairer and fouler," a surprisingly blunt part of the contract that reminded couples of the role that fate sometimes played in the marriage "bet.")

Back then, people who committed adultery were known as *wed-breaks*. I guess that means they welched on the bet. *Welching* on a bet, of course, means ignoring your obligation to pay. This verb *to welch* seems to come from an insult the English leveled against the Welsh, suggesting unreliability when it came to paying their debts.

With the low success rate of weddings today, it's probably best to just go to Vegas and find something to gamble on instead. You'll probably end up saving money!

White wedding dresses became popular during the Victorian era because the Victorians thought the color white . . .

A. was a symbol of the innocence of childhood
B. was a symbol of virginity
C. matched up well with almost any other color
D. protected the bride from being seduced by the devil

(Answer: a)

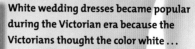

Hot for Words/Sex Ed

47

4TH PERIOD

History

Fully Exposed

America

Many people wonder why America was not named after Christopher Columbus, but instead after some later explorer named Amerigo Vespucci. Who was this Amerigo guy, and why does his name get to be the inspiration for not one, but two continent names—North America and South America—when we could be talking about North and South Columbia instead?

ACTUALLY, COLUMBUS WASN'T even the first European to reach what would eventually be called the "Americas." The Norse explorer Leif Eriksson came before him by about five hundred years, and there may have been more explorers before that. Vespucci, who landed in the New World after both Eriksson and Columbus, had two things going for him: a better sense of geography and the ability to write interesting letters back home. Vespucci proved that the place where Columbus had landed was not an adjoining part of Asia, but a whole new continent—the fourth to be discovered, or so he thought at the time.

More important, his letters back home were both exciting and widely circulated, and it appears to have been because of Vespucci's journeys that Europeans started talking about a whole new continent. The letters made for sensational reading, painting a picture of a land populated by sexually voracious females who had no qualms about moving from one partner to another when they got bored. This was gripping stuff—much more intriguing than anything Columbus had sent home about the land he thought was India.

It was because of these letters that Amerigo Vespucci was on the mind of the German mapmaker in charge of coming up with a name for the new continents in 1507. This mapmaker used a feminized Latin form of Vespucci's first name: *America*. Good thing, too. Otherwise, we might be living in the United States of Leifia . . . or North Christopheria! Neither quite sounds right.

After two voyages to the lands that came to bear his name, Amerigo Vespucci was rewarded with a special, highly paid post that had been created especially for him. What was it?

A. Chief Mapmaker to King Ferdinand
B. Pilot Major of Spain
C. Inspector of Public Morals in the New World
D. Official Namer of New Continents

(Answer: b)

Amazon

It's the name of a river. It's the name of an online bookstore. It's even a kind of parrot you can find in South America. But where in the world did the word *Amazon* come from in the first place?

THE WORD ORIGINALLY REFERRED to a race of warrior women who supposedly thrived in the ancient region known as Scythia. *Amazon* was given by the Greek historian Herodotus, among others, as the tribal name of these fierce females.

Herodotus is today known as the "Father of History," but, consciously or unconsciously, he appears to have stretched the truth just a little when he passed along his amazing *Amazon* accounts. He claimed that the warrior women were so bent on victory that in order to fire arrows more efficiently, they each cauterized their right breast in order to keep it from developing. In Greek, *a-* meant "without" and *-mazon* meant "breast."

Whether or not he knew it, what Herodotus was passing along may have been an old piece of folk etymology. Some people believe that the name *Amazon* may have been inspired by the foreign phrase *ha-mazan*, which would translate in Iranian as "fighting together." To the Greeks, however, this word would have sounded like "A-mazon"—meaning "breastless." It's possible someone made up the story of the women who cut off their own breasts to make the foreign-sounding word make more sense—in Greek. Or maybe someone was just looking for a good story to tell.

Herodotus called these warriors "man-killers." Scary stuff for men! The question is: Did the Amazons actually exist? People have taken them very seriously for many centuries, but the best evidence now is that they were nervous figments of the (male) imagination, always threatening the civilized order . . . and always located in some ambiguous territory beyond the borderline, somewhere "out there."

The Amazon River in South America was so named because . . .

A. only one-breasted women are allowed to swim there

B. it is the easiest place in the world to buy books about the legendary Amazons

C. Spanish conquistadors were attacked there by women warriors who reminded them of the legendary Amazons

D. the river was described by an American explorer as "amazin' "—and a version of the name stuck

(Answer: c)

In what year did Captain Boycott have such an unpleasant time with the Irish Land League?

A. 1050
B. 1980
C. 870
D. 1880

(Answer: d. This was the same year that Helen Keller was born and the first electric streetlight in the United States was installed in Wabash, Indiana.)

Boycott

AS WITH ALL THESE LESSONS on history, there is a story to tell here. An English military man, Captain Charles Cunningham Boycott, took up residence in County Mayo, Ireland, in service of the Earl of Erne. Boycott worked as a land agent, and part of his job was to inform the locals that their rents had been raised.

This news did not always go over well. The community organized against Boycott, and found numerous ways to make his life unpleasant. For instance, they kept Boycott from receiving his mail. They blockaded his home, which meant his food deliveries stopped. And they refused to sell him anything. Boycott eventually had to go back to England. Ever since, the practice of using economic and social leverage to make life miserable for a person, company, or nation has been known as a *boycott*. The word refers specifically to the practice of refusing to do business with the targeted party, but can also mean, as it did in Boycott's case, a larger refusal to have anything to do with someone or something, as a form of protest.

I think it's interesting that the verb *boycott* now describes the action of protesting by means of economic and social isolation, whereas originally Boycott himself was the victim of the practice. He probably would have described the process a little differently, and I doubt that he took much pleasure in having his name connected with the tactic.

There are three lessons to draw from this word: First, if you're a landlord, think twice before you raise the rent. Second, if you are bound and determined to do something unpopular to a group of Irish people, don't send an Englishman to announce it. Third, don't be surprised if the English language appropriates your name without prior notice. If you're not careful, you might just end up in the dictionary.

The term "male chauvinist pig" was first used . . .

A. by feminists in the 1970s to describe certain self-absorbed men

B. in the movie *Mary Poppins* to describe Mr. Banks

C. to describe a certain breed of pig that exhibited unruly behavior

D. by Yale University sorority girls to describe certain fraternity brothers on their campus

(Answer: a)

Chauvinist

We're familiar with this word from the seventies catchphrase "male chauvinist pig"—but what exactly is a *chauvinist*? Could there ever be a female one? If you are a *chauvinist*, are you also, by definition, a pig?

IT TURNS OUT that there was a soldier named Nicholas Chauvin during the era of Napoleon whose love and admiration for his commander endured long beyond Napoleon's final defeat at Waterloo. This soldier, who had been wounded in battle many times, was so eager to praise the deposed military dictator that he actually made people laugh, and eventually became a target of scorn and satire.

Because of Chauvin's fixation on the idea that Napoleon had been the right guy to follow, the word *chauvinism* emerged as a description of someone with fierce, but misguided, patriotic values. It eventually picked up a parallel meaning, namely the attitude that commits excessive, unreasoning loyalty to a certain viewpoint, cause, or even a certain gender.

So yes, there could be (and in fact are) female chauvinists. That would be someone who regards men as inherently inferior to women, and holds to that way of thinking no matter what.

The "pig" thing is just name-calling. People of both genders do it. But you knew that.

Personally, I wish we could all just kiss and make up. Don't you?

Philander

SOME BASHFUL DICTIONARIES will tell you that the verb *to philander* simply means "to flirt," but others are less squeamish. American Heritage acknowledges that it means what most people who actually use the word think it means, namely, "to carry on a sexual affair, especially an extramarital affair, with a woman one cannot or does not intend to marry." It goes on to point out that the word is used exclusively to describe the behavior of men.

A woman who engages in such activities is more likely to be described—though probably not to her face—as a *hussy* (see p. 45). It's interesting to me that the word *philanderer* incorporates the idea that the promiscuous male can't or won't consider marriage, whereas the promiscuous female might.

But where did this word originate? The English playwright William Congreve named a character Philander in his 1700 play *The Way of the World*. The name actually comes from *philandros,* meaning "man-loving" in Greek, which I don't think is what Congreve had in mind. The name *Philander* has been used to describe (heterosexual) male romantic leads in stories and fables since at least the Middle Ages. The use of *philandering* to describe an excessively casual attitude toward "woman-loving" dates back to the mid-nineteenth century. The modern sense almost always carries the meaning of "male serial adulterer," which (let's face it) goes quite a bit beyond flirting.

Philander Chase Knox was . . .

A. the pseudonym of a 1980s porn star

B. the hero of a novel by Emily Brontë

C. attorney general of the United States under Theodore Roosevelt

D. a pet name for John F. Kennedy bestowed on him by one of his White House intimates

(Answer: c)

Tantalize

THIS WORD DERIVES FROM the Greek god and king of Phrygia named Tantalus—who, the story goes, got on Zeus's bad side and had to pay the price. As punishment for getting Zeus angry, Tantalus was placed in water up to his chin and held there immobile—as luscious fruits hung down from a nearby tree, seemingly just within nibbling range. Whenever he tried to bite the delicious fruit, it moved away; whenever he tried to drink the water that surrounded him, it receded. So the word *tantalize,* from this story, came to mean the act of tormenting someone by seeming to offer him something he could never, in a million years, actually possess.

In modern usage, *to tantalize* means to let a person see something that's alluring or capable of provoking strong desire—but never actually giving it to him.

What a terrible form of torture!

Tantalus's big sin was . . .

A. stealing ambrosia and revealing the secrets of the gods
B. serving his son as food to the god Demeter
C. stealing a golden dog
D. any one of the above—the Greeks told many versions of the same story

(Answer: d)

Vandal

We all know what vandalism is: the act of destroying or defacing someone else's property, especially the act of deliberately messing up public property or cultural artifacts, more or less for the fun of it. But did you know that the name comes from a tribe of real-life Vandals who attacked the Roman Empire in the fifth century A.D.?

THE VANDALS WERE A GERMANIC TRIBE that took advantage of a series of political, military, and diplomatic mistakes to sack Rome in the year 455. These Vandals seem to have gotten a particularly bad rap, though, considering that they weren't the only people who raided the city during the long, ugly period when Rome was getting flabby and complacent, and they didn't do all *that* much damage for damage's sake—at least not compared to some of the other great pillagers of history. The Vandals did make off with the treasures of the Temple of Jerusalem, it's true, but the Romans had stolen them in the first place, so they weren't really in a position to complain too loudly about it.

In the centuries that followed the Vandals' big rip-off, some historians who pined for the good old days of the Roman Empire used them as an example of the kind of wanton, senseless destruction of culture that separates civilized people from the lower types. In fact, though, the early Vandals seem to have been much more interested in finding and keeping valuable items than they were in destroying Roman statues and monuments for recreational purposes. Contemporary vandals get more of a kick out of damaging property than preserving anything.

Give me the real Vandals over the modern vandals any day.

Vandal comes from the Proto-Germanic word *Wandal*, which means . . .

A. destroyer
B. wrecker
C. wanderer
D. thief

(Answer: c. This was the tribe's own name for themselves.)

nickers

Here we have a word that means one of two very different things, depending on whether you are American or British.

Both meanings connect to a shortened form of the proper name *Knickerbocker*, which translates literally to "marble baker," though no Dutch were known for baking marbles!

THE NAME IS NOT ONLY fun to say but also fun to explain. In the 1600s, early Dutch colonists settled in the region of New Amsterdam, now known as New York City. A few hundred years later, they were depicted in an illustrated 1859 book as people who wore really big, loose-fitting pants. Cartoonists tend to exaggerate things—especially a couple of centuries after the fact—but the Dutch of early New York, some of whom were named Knickerbocker, did actually wear pretty baggy trousers, even by modern-day standards. The funny name latched on to the funny pants at some point in the nineteenth century, and *knickers* entered the lexicon.

If you are American, *knickers* means the kind of short, slightly baggy trousers that golfers wore back in the thirties. If you are capable of picturing the Three Stooges playing golf, you

TRUE OR FALSE

Due to the influence of the Dutch in early New York City, one of the first baseball teams in New York City was called the New York Knickerbockers.

ANSWER True. An early version of baseball's official rules was known as the Knickerbocker Rules. Later on, the New York Knickerbockers—or "Knicks"—basketball team took the name.

are probably capable of picturing this variety of knickers, and just as capable of quickly moving on to some more interesting subject.

If you are British, though, *knickers* means a loose-fitting undergarment, often made of silk, that is designed to cover the anatomical region located between, say, the navel and the upper thigh of the human female. If you have just now pictured Grace Kelly, in her prime, wearing such a garment, and no other, the odds are good that you are male, you do not want to go back to picturing the Three Stooges on the golf course, and you are beginning to prefer the British interpretation.

The phrase "getting one's knickers in a twist" connects to the British meaning. It means "to become agitated, anxious, or disoriented." As for me, I never get my knickers in a twist.

Siren

THIS WORD ORIGINALLY MEANT—and still means —"a sea nymph whose alluring song leads sailors to their doom." Sirens are usually depicted either as having the body of a bird or the body of a fish, but they always have the head of a human female. Homer's masterpiece *The Odyssey* tells of Odysseus's intense desire to hear the famous voices of the Sirens. He had himself tied securely to the mast and ordered his men to plug their ears with wax so they couldn't hear the otherworldly beauty of the Sirens' song. Odysseus and his crew thankfully survived. The name appears to derive from an old Greek word meaning "rope" or "cord."

Today, the word *siren* also describes the wailing up-and-down lament of the police cruiser or the steamship: a different kind of song, to be sure, but one still (at least potentially) associated with danger and death.

TRUE OR FALSE

Sirens are sometimes represented as mermaids.

ANSWER True. Both serve as symbols of danger and transformation in Western culture. The Starbucks logo is a Siren, though of what impending danger she is warning us, I have no idea!

Lunchtime

Mouthwatering

Milk

Got milk? Most of us do—and probably would whether or not there had ever been a big ad campaign urging us to go out and buy some at the supermarket.

CONSUMING MILK FROM COWS AND GOATS—and, of course, people—has been a central part of the human experience for quite some time, so it is not at all surprising that the English word *milk* is one of those very old members of the word club. Like *God, love, king, queen, blood,* and, yes, *breast, milk* dates back to a time long before the Romans had anything to do with the growth and development of our language. These are all Anglo-Saxon members of the family. In Old English, we said *meoluc* for *milk; meoluc* derived from an ancient root that came from various Old Norse, Dutch, and German verbs meaning "to stroke," referring, of course, to the hand motion that is essential to milking an animal. Picture someone milking a cow and stroking the udder until the milk comes forth. That's the basic idea behind the verb we're talking about here.

Of course, there are a lot of applications. The idea of milking someone or something for material advantage—that is, stroking until you attain some figurative, rather than literal, form of nourishment—dates back to the sixteenth century.

The same ancient root also appears to have inspired Latin forms that eventually gave us words like *promulgate,* meaning to make something widely known—by spreading (an announcement) far and wide. Look carefully at *promulgate* and you will see that old verb *meoluc* meaning "to cause to emerge by stroking." Thus, someone who *promulgates* a message is, well, *disseminating* it. That's another body metaphor. Go look it up for yourself.

Which of the following words does not derive, directly or indirectly, from the same ancient word root as milk?

A. milch
B. emulsion
C. malcontent
D. liebfraumilch

(Answer: C)

Hamburger and Frankfurter

THE HAMBURGER IS NAMED AFTER the German city of Hamburg, a major port that owes its association with the American meat sandwich to German immigrants. The center of the sandwich was a ground-meat preparation that had been popular for centuries in Germany, and was thus known as a *Hamburg steak* in nineteenth-century America. Occasionally the dish was known as a *hamburg* or a *hamburger sandwich,* but eventually *hamburger* won out. That's about as much information as anyone has been able to track down for sure about the etymology of the dish we call a *hamburger.* Many people claim to have invented the hamburger, but there's no one definitive creator.

The popular suffix *-burger* has a much better documented history, as the element denoting various types of hamburger. This suffix yielded *cheeseburger* in the late 1930s, *beefburger* in 1940 (apparently an attempt to make it clear that the dish did not use pork), and, in a stunning and unprecedented testament to truth in advertising, the *Fatburger* in 1952, which is still sold at the Southern California eateries of the same name. Modern variations on the *-burger* include *fishburger* and *soyburger*.

Interestingly, the other major point of protein worship in the modern American fast-food meal system, the *frankfurter*, also gets its name from a German city. The enterprising butchers of Frankfurt promoted a particular variety of spiced sausage in the middle of the nineteenth century, which was successfully marketed by street vendors in New York City in the early years of the twentieth century. Today, we still call these sausages *frankfurters*, but we are much more likely to call them "hot dogs."

The reason for this new label is that college students in the late 1800s actually thought that the frankfurters were made from dog meat! It may have started out as a joke, but it eventually caught on. Surprisingly, the industry adopted the name and to this day continues to call them "hot dogs"! And you can still get them on many street corners in New York City.

A similar xenophobic sentiment—this time directed at the French in 2003 for their lack of support for the United States' invasion of Iraq—caused which restaurant to change the name of its "French Fries" to "Freedom Fries"?

A. McDonald's
B. Wendy's
C. Restaurants and cafés run by the U.S. House of Representatives
D. Jack in the Box

(Answer: c. The name change also applied to their "French Toast." "French Fries" and "French Toast" returned to the menu in 2006.)

Artichoke

I just love artichokes. Don't you? Recently, someone asked me: "Did the first guy who ate an artichoke choke on it?" Interesting question!

THE WORD *ARTICHOKE* DATES BACK to a story in which King Arthur was served the exotic vegetable. Not realizing the he was not supposed to eat the spiny husks, he choked on it, and died. Get it? Arthur? Choke? According to this story, that was the original name for this food: the Arthur Choke, later shortened to Artie Choke, then artichoke. Another mystery solved.

Actually, not so much. If you believed that business about King Arthur and the unfamiliar vegetable, I suspect that you will, like Arthur and unlike me, swallow anything.

In reality, the *artichoke* gets its name from the Arabians. They thought the plant resembled a thistle, so that's what they called it: the thistle, which in Arabic is *al-kharshuf*. When this phrase was transferred into Spanish, it became *alcarchofa*, then *alcochofa*, then *articiocco* in Italian, and, eventually, *artichock* in English. So how did *-choke*, which is derived from the Old English word *aceocian,* get attached at the end? It looks like *choke* may have actually been influenced by the fact that someone, at some point, believed the prickly vegetable was named because someone had choked on it. So even though I made the first story up, it's partially true, and why today we eat artichokes instead of "artichocks."

Which of these modern words do etymologists believe is related to the same Old English word as the modern word *choke*?

A. joke
B. jerk
C. chalk
D. cheek

(Answer: d)

Eggs Benedict

TRUE STORY: Back in 1894, there was a playboy named Samuel Benedict who lived in New York City. One afternoon, after a long, eventful, and only dimly remembered night of partying, he woke up with a powerful hangover. He walked carefully and purposefully into the Waldorf-Astoria Hotel on 34th Street, where he ordered a high-protein meal that he hoped would still the ringing in his ears, subdue the pain in his skull, and remind him of the three familiar dimensions he knew he had once been accustomed to navigating.

That meal—bacon, two poached eggs, and buttered toast, which Benedict slathered in hollandaise sauce—caught the attention of the maître d', who promptly instructed that it be placed on the hotel menu as "eggs Benedict." (For the record, *egg* is an Old Norse word for the food product we boil, scramble, and poach.) The hotel made a couple of cosmetic changes, replacing the toast with an English muffin and the bacon with a slice of ham.

History does not record whether the dish actually relieved Benedict's hangover, but I hope it did.

The first documented use of the word "hangover" to describe the aftereffects of a drinking binge dates from . . .

A. the 1600s
B. the 1700s
C. the 1800s
D. the 1900s

(Answer: d—1904, to be precise. So Benedict probably would have used some other word to describe his sorry condition on the day he dragged himself into the Waldorf-Astoria.)

Humble Pie

Brace yourself. I am afraid this one is a little disgusting.

BACK IN THE MIDDLE AGES, you really didn't want to be part of the servant class, especially when it came to dinner. Nowadays, if you decide that it makes sense to take a job as a waitress, you still can buy your own decent meal somewhere. Eight hundred years ago, if you were serving dinner to m'lord and m'lady, they got all the good cuts of meat, while you got the "skin, head, shoulders, and umbles." *Umbles*, in this case, meant the entrails of the animal being eaten. So there really was a dish called *umble pie,* which was a pie whose filling was . . . um . . . intestines. Yecch.

Not surprisingly, the phrase "eating umble pie" came to be associated with the "humble" station that inferiors held in relation to their superiors. So "eating humble pie" eventually came to mean "abasing oneself."

But not so fast. *Umble* isn't where the modern word *humble* came from. *Humble* derives from the Latin word *humilis,* meaning literally "of the earth," or, by extension, "lowly." This version of *humble* can be found in English as early as the thirteenth century. The nasty *umble pie* people really ate arrived about four centuries later, and the expression *humble pie* seems to have showed up in the first half of the nineteenth century.

Humble Pie was also . . .

A. an English supergroup from the 1970s
B. a delicacy among the French
C. a dessert using the spleen of a camel
D. none of the above

(Answer: a)

Science

The Laws of Attraction

Dr. Sexy

TRUE OR FALSE

The milk-producing glands of mammals are evolutionarily modified sweat glands.

ANSWER True.

Mammal

MAMMALS, YOUR GRADE-SCHOOL biology textbook informed you tactfully, are those animals that possess certain common characteristics: fur or hair, warm blood, a backbone, et cetera. That "et cetera" certainly covered a lot of territory, didn't it? Don't get me wrong: The hair, the blood, the spinal column, even certain intricate parallels in inner ear development—these are all very interesting commonalities among mammals. Yet they are all definitely sideshows when compared to the main attraction: breasts.

Breasts (or "milk-secreting organs," as one of my sources decorously puts it) capable of feeding the young are the chief dividing line separating mammals from other classes of animals, and the critical thing we mammals have in common, at least as far as the females are concerned. The etymology reflects this fearlessly: *Mammal* comes from the Latin words *mamma,* meaning "breast," and *mammalis,* meaning "of the breast." Human beings, as primates, definitely qualify.

The word mamma itself seems to come from the sound a baby makes when breast feeding.

Mammals with more than two breasts are said to have *dugs* instead, which doesn't sound half as romantic. This word has no relation to the vernacular *jugs*, which also can kill the mood, and which comes to us by means of a colorful Australian term for human female breasts: "milk jugs."

Hermaphrodite

THIS WORD IS USED TO DESCRIBE an organism possessing, or capable of possessing, both male and female reproductive organs. Many species incorporate some form of hermaphrodite sexuality within their life cycle. One example is the clownfish, the male of which can switch genders if no females are to be found. (That's something they didn't show you in *Finding Nemo*.)

The word *hermaphrodite* derives from classical sources. According to the poet and "master of love" Ovid, who adapted an old Greek myth, Hermaphroditus was the son of the deities Aphrodite and Hermes, and an object of obsession for the nymph Salmacis. Salmacis prayed to be united forever with Hermaphroditus; her prayer was granted, and the two were fused into a single being, thus combining male and female traits.

The myth has resonated down the centuries, and the term *hermaphrodite* was used to describe people with male and female reproductive organs. Starting in 1910, the term *intersex* was created as an alternate and many people prefer this term over *hermaphrodite*.

Which poet followed in Ovid's footsteps and wrote about the myth of Hermaphroditus and Salmacis?

A.   Ted Hughes
B.   Allen Ginsberg
C.   Algernon Swinburne
D.   all of the above

(Answer: c)

Which of the following actors has not played Batman's archenemy, the Joker?

A. Jack Nicholson
B. Heath Ledger
C. Arnold Schwarzenegger
D. Cesar Romero

(Answer: c. Nicholson played the role in the 1989 film *Batman*, Ledger in 2008's *The Dark Knight*, and Romero in the 1966 film version.)

Coulrophobia

(If you really suffer from coulrophobia, you've probably already decided to skip this one.)

DID YOU KNOW THAT some people have an overwhelming fear of clowns? It's not a joke—phobias are real mental roadblocks, and they are often completely debilitating to the people who suffer from them. Some people have exaggerated fears of heights, or of spiders, or even of the number thirteen. The words for those conditions are *acrophobia*, *arachnophobia*, and *triskaidekaphobia*, respectively. You may have already guessed that the *-phobia* part means "fear" in Greek, and the first half of each word is the Greek word for whatever the person is afraid of: *acro-* for heights or summits, *arachno-* for spiders, and *triskaideka-* for thirteen.

So *coulro-* must mean "clown" in Greek, right? Actually, it doesn't. *Coulro-* is connected to the Greek word *kolon*, meaning "limb," which only deepens the mystery . . . until you realize that the Greek word *kolobathristes* means "stilt-walker"—someone who walks on limbs. Maybe people who walked on stilts painted their faces back in the old days.

The point is, people who suffer from *coulrophobia* aren't putting on an act. They're really terrified, and they spend more time being terrified than you might think. Just think of all the images that have flooded through global media channels over the years of Batman's archenemy the Joker, and you'll start to have a sense of what they have to deal with.

The word *coulrophobia* is only about twenty years old and therefore doesn't appear in too many dictionaries yet, perhaps because most people are still unaware of this condition. But the condition appears to be real. You can see for yourself on my website at www.hotforwords.com/fearofclowns.

The Partridge Family was ...

A. a team of trained birds that broke wind on cue for circus promoter P. T. Barnum

B. a Christmas crèche that was ruled acceptable by the United States Supreme Court in 1973 because it had no overt religious symbolism

C. a musical TV family from the late 1960s featuring actress Shirley Jones, teen heartthrob David Cassidy, and the always colorful Danny Bonaduce

D. a figment of our collective imagination

(Answer: c)

Partridge

What, specifically, do you think of when you think of the partridge? If you're like most of us, you think of the Christmas carol *The Twelve Days of Christmas*. In the lyrics to that song, which date back to at least 1780, the "partridge in a pear tree" is the first in a series of increasingly extravagant gifts, each bestowed on one of the twelve days between the Christian holidays of Christmas and Epiphany.

IT'S NOT VERY LIKELY that "partridge" made you think of farting—but that is what the Greeks thought of when they named the partridge thousands of years ago. The bird's moniker derives from the Greek word *perdix*, which means "a person who breaks wind." The whirring sound of the bird's wings apparently evoked a gastric sound for the Greeks. The bird was known in English as the *patrich*, and then eventually as the *partridge*. People who hunt them confirm that the bird does apparently make such a sound as it flies.

A little tidbit you can use to break the ice at the next office holiday party.

Giraffe

THIS NAME FOR THE ANIMAL with a remarkably long neck has interested me for a long time, because it is essentially the same in both Russian and English (and a lot of other languages), which is rare. For a long time, though, the giraffe went by another, and I think much more interesting, name: *camelopard*.

That's what the Romans called it, because the animal's height and long neck reminded them of the camel, and its spots reminded them of the leopard. Seems logical enough, doesn't it? And it's fun to say, too: "camelopard."

That cool, logical name was eventually replaced by the word *giraffe*, which may have been derived from an ambiguous Arabic word: *zirafa*. Today, nobody with a degree and a reputation in the world of etymology seems willing to comment in public on what this word *zirafa* actually meant. It must be some kind of state secret.

The Italians apparently turned *zirafa* into *giraffa*, which made it into English as *giraffe* around the end of the sixteenth century, and there ends my short story about the animal with the long neck—except to point out that the compound *camelopard* was still in circulation in England well into the 1800s.

How many hours does a giraffe need to sleep in a 24-hour period?

A. ten hours
B. eighteen hours
C. eight hours
D. two hours

(Answer: d—2 hours! I wish I could function on that little sleep!)

Pupil

Isn't a pupil the opening in your iris that lets light pass into your eye? Of course. So how does it also refer to a person who is being taught by a teacher?

PUPIL COMES FROM the Latin words *pupus,* meaning little boy, and *pupa,* meaning little girl. Since small children are usually in the learning stage, it gradually came to refer to a small child being taught something.

Okay. That explains the student part, but what about the reference to the eye? For that, we need to look a little deeper. Are you ready?

Look very closely . . . no, not at me! Look into your own eye in the mirror. What do you see? Stare at the black part of the eye, and then look at what's inside. You should see your own reflection. You might even think of it as a smaller version of yourself, like a small child or a doll. People started referring to the dark opening part of the eye as a *pupil* because when you look into it, you see a small reflection of yourself.

WHO SAID THIS?

"Self-knowledge can be obtained only by looking into the mind and virtue of the soul, which is the diviner part of a man, as we see our own image in another's eye."

- A. Mahatma Gandhi
- B. Plato
- C. Ralph Waldo Emerson
- D. Bill O'Reilly

(Answer: b)

- Mahatma Gandhi said, "An eye for an eye only ends up making the whole world blind."

- Ralph Waldo Emerson said, "The sun illuminates only the eye of the man, but shines into the eye and the heart of the child."

- Bill O'Reilly said, "The children of America have seen with their own eyes that liars can win and cheaters can prosper. They know that our nation will accept venal behavior and, in some cases, reward it with tremendous wealth and power. So why wouldn't they lie, cheat, and steal?"

Who wrote this?

O devil, devil!
If that the earth could teem with woman's tears,
Each drop she falls would prove a crocodile.
Out of my sight!

    A. William Shakespeare
    B. Ben Jonson
    C. Christopher Marlowe
    A. Thomas Kyd

(Answer: a—William Shakespeare, in *Othello*.)

Crocodile Tears

THE WORD *CROCODILE* comes from two old Greek words: *kroke*, meaning "gravel," and *drilos*, meaning "worm." The Greeks saw the *crocodile* and thought it looked like a big worm that crawled through gravel—hence the name.

Ancient Greek and Roman stories gave people the idea that the crocodile shed tears in order to attract the attention and assistance of passing human beings, whom the beasts then devoured. It isn't true, but it has made a good story for the past couple of millennia. For at least the last six hundred years, English-speaking writers have made reference to the story, usually because it helped them to convey the idea of "false concern for another person" or "inauthentic grief" in a way that was easy to remember. And that's what the phrase "crocodile tears" means today: an expression of sorrow, grief, or empathy for another person that isn't really genuine. Actually, though, the act of pretending to be sorry for someone—when you really aren't sorry at all—seems to be an exclusively human trait. There's no need to bring the crocodile's reputation down for something we do and it doesn't.

Some people will try to tell you that the reason the belief about crocodiles crying is a myth is that crocodiles don't have tear ducts. They actually do, but they don't use them to lure people into snapping range.

Oxygen

This is a word that seems to have been around forever, but hasn't. Like a lot of interesting words, *oxygen* is based on a misunderstanding.

OXYGEN COMES FROM the French *oxygène*, which the great scientist Antoine-Laurent Lavoisier coined in 1777 from a Greek front half (*oxys*, meaning "sharp or acidic") and a French back half (*-gène*, meaning "that which produces"). In other words, Lavoisier thought that oxygen itself was a constituent of all acids.

Not so, but don't give him too much grief for making that mistake. Lavoisier did carry out the first definitive experiments in oxidation, correctly explained the phenomenon of combustion, and proved that the substance we now know by the name he gave it—*oxygen*—was actually a chemical element, not simply an altered form of air. By the way, "air" means simply that portion of the atmosphere humans breathe; oxygen gas makes up about 20% of the Earth's atmosphere.

Take a deep breath . . . and consider that all living organisms, including the body you are using to breathe, contain molecular structures that use oxygen, whatever name it goes by. Here's my advice regarding oxygen: When in doubt, breathe in and out deeply. It makes things much more vivid. Must be the extra oxygen.

Lavoisier's contemporary Joseph Priestley had a different name for oxygen. What was it?

A. O_2
B. Air Supply
C. dephlogisticated air
D. phlogisticated air

(Answer: c. This means that the air lacked phlogiston, an imaginary substance that was released when something burned, later discovered not to exist.)

7TH PERIOD

Debate Club

Urban Legends

 John Wilkes Booth had a relative who earned much more praise than he ever did, and who had nothing to do with assaulting the president. Identify that relative.

- A. Jodie Foster
- B. Isadora Duncan
- C. Edwin Booth
- D. Joan Collins

(Answer: c. He was one of the most acclaimed Shakespearean actors of his day.)

"Break a Leg"

Maybe you're as puzzled as I am whenever you hear someone say "break a leg" when they mean to wish another person good luck. Why would it be a good thing to break your leg? There are many legends connected to this phrase, but here's the most common one:

IN THE OLD DAYS, they would raise and lower the theater curtain with a wooden crank, called a *leg*. If you had a *really* good performance, there would be so many encores that the curtain would be raised and lowered so often that as a result, the leg crank would break. Hence the expression, "break a leg."

A less popular, but equally interesting urban legend is that when President Abraham Lincoln was assassinated in 1865, the man who shot him, actor John Wilkes Booth, leaped from the president's private box, landed on the stage twenty or so feet below, and broke his leg. Ever since, when actors have wanted to wish each other luck, they've said "break a leg," though I still can't figure out the logic on this one.

Where the expression most likely came from is the Hebrew expression *hatzlakha u-brakha*, which means "Success and Blessing." The Germans borrowed that expression, but rather than putting in German words that had the same meaning, they instead used words that sounded similar, and they ended up with *Hals und Beinbruch*, which means "neck and leg break" in German.

When the Germans came to America around 1930, they translated that expression into English (using the meaning this time, not what it sounded like) and we ended up with the "break a leg" that we have today.

"His Name Is Mud"

"HIS NAME IS MUD" INDICATES that the person is not too popular, or that people are upset with him. The too-good-to-be-true legend behind this one goes as follows: While on the run from the law, John Wilkes Booth (yes, him again) got help from a physician named Samuel Mudd. Mudd tended to the busted ankle Booth got as a result of jumping from the balcony of Ford's Theater.

Mudd was caught and sentenced to life in prison for aiding Lincoln's assassin. Ever since, people who have found themselves in imminent, unavoidably deep trouble have been compared to Dr. Mudd—by means of the phrase, "His name is mud."

Okay, everything you just read about John Wilkes Booth and Dr. Samuel Mudd is true—*except* for the part about Mudd's name originating the phrase, "His name is mud." There are a couple of tip-offs to consider here. First of all, there's a *d* missing in "mud." Second of all, the phrase, "His name is mud," shows up in print at least forty-five years earlier with precisely the same meaning. People didn't bother making up an elaborate explanation for the phrase at the time, though, because in the early eighteenth century, *mud* meant about the same thing that words like *idiot* or *dope* mean to us today— the lowest form of anything. When someone said your name was mud, what they meant was that you were an idiot, a dope.

Today it also means that you are in trouble for pissing people off, perhaps influenced by the Samuel Mudd folk etymology.

Dr. Samuel Mudd was . . .

A. eventually pardoned by President Andrew Johnson

B. deprived of prison privileges because he attempted to escape

C. convinced to take on the role of prison doctor in the federal facility where he was held after the death of the official prison doctor during a severe yellow fever epidemic

D. all of the above

(Answer: d, all of the above, but not in that order.)

A kangaroo court is so called because . . .

A. it's a kind of court that originated in Australia
B. it always results in a verdict of innocent, and baby kangaroos—*joeys*—are the most innocent thing imaginable
C. it leaps forward to its outcome quickly
D. it was the kind of court over which Captain James Cook presided

(Answer: C. A kangaroo court is an improperly constituted court where the outcome is determined prior to the trial.)

Kangaroo

ACCORDING TO LEGEND, English sea captain James Cook, while in Australia in the 1700s, saw a kangaroo loping by and asked a native to tell him what the strange creature was called. The reply came back: "kangaroo"—and Cook dutifully recorded this name. Europeans quickly adopted it once he made it back home and shared what he had seen. What Cook didn't know, however, was that the word the native had shared with him simply meant, "I don't know what you're talking about." So it was that the kangaroo got its distinctive name from a simple failure to communicate.

Or at least, that's the story people love to circulate. As you know by now, in the world of etymology we have learned from experience that great stories are usually reasons for great caution. This version of the Cook story is (as you probably have guessed by now) untrue. I wish the truth weren't a hundred times more boring, but it is. Cook did in fact take down the word "kangaroo," and he did indeed circulate the name and the description of the remarkable animal he had seen.

People in Europe also traveled to Australia years later and tried to find the word *kangaroo* in any of the Australian dialects, but were unsuccessful. Since they never found the word anywhere on the island, people developed the tale we heard earlier, and that legend remained for some three hundred years, until 1971 when a scientist finally found the original tribe that had uttered the word to Cook, thus ruining one of the greatest etymology stories of our time. In the end, the kangaroo got its name from the word *kangaroo*. Oh well . . . time to make some more stories up!

OK

My dear students, you may at some point hear some absurd explanations for this popular two-letter phrase meaning "acceptable or very good."

ONE OF THE MOST COMMONLY CIRCULATED STORIES suggests that the expression is rooted in the American president Andrew Jackson's inability to spell. In this story, Jackson supposedly used this abbreviation when he wanted to leave a notation on a document signifying that it was "oll korrect." Yeah, right. Since when does the president of the United States spend his time proofreading things? I don't know how good a speller Andrew Jackson was, but I don't think that's how *OK* became OK to use as an expression of approval or support, or (in verb form) how we came to "okay" things.

The most persuasive story does connect to a U.S. president,

Okily-dokily is a variant of *OK* popularized by . . .

A. Ned Flanders on the television show *The Simpsons*

B. talk show host David Letterman

C. President Andrew Jackson

D. yours truly

(Answer: a)

though. When future commander in chief Martin Van Buren was practicing law in New York State, he earned the nickname "The Red Fox of Kinderhook." That's because he was born in, and practiced law in, a town called Old Kinderhook. Around the same time, Boston newspapers were involved in a fad of abbreviating expressions, especially misspelling them as "country bumpkins" would supposedly do, and "O.K." was an abbreviation for "oll korrect." Influenced by this fad, Van Buren's supporters used the initials of Van Buren's hometown, and named the club that promoted and supported Van Buren's political views the O.K. Club. They would chant that the O.K. Club was "oll korrect" or "all right."

The initials O.K., eventually rendered as *OK* and *okay,* started out in life as a fad in Boston newspapers, commandeered as a political slogan in support of Van Buren, and from there became popular as an expression of approval or enthusiasm.

There are many contenders for the origin of *OK*; this is the one I'm willing to okay, OK?

The writer H. L. Mencken considered *OK* "the most shining and successful Americanism ever invented."

"Rule of Thumb"

There's a very common story that the phrase "rule of thumb" originated from an old English law that permitted a man to beat his wife—as long as he used a stick or rod that was no wider than his own thumb. I had to investigate this one.

THE PHRASE CAN BE TRACED back to 1692, and it's gone through some changes of meaning since then. Today, the phrase "rule of thumb" refers to things you know from experience: not to let milk boil, not to leave knives out where children can get at them, not to sleep with someone on the first date. It can also refer to informal guidelines or standards. But what do thumbs have to do with any of this?

There actually was no law permitting men to beat their wives, with a rod or anything else, back in 1692. In fact, this kind of assault was as illegal then as it is now. The original meaning of the phrase "rule of thumb" had nothing to do with the legal "rules" governing interactions between the sexes. Instead, it had to do with the kind of "rule" that's all about measuring things—the same root that gives us the word *ruler*. The phrase "rule of thumb" became popular because the first joint of an adult human thumb, when you measure it, is usually pretty close to being one inch long. Not *exactly* one inch long, mind you, but close. (Find a ruler and see for yourself.) If you didn't happen to have a ruler around, you could use the "rule of thumb."

Eventually, the weird story about the law permitting a man to beat his wife influenced the meaning of the phrase, as rule of thumb no longer referred so much to measuring things, but to learning by experience. And, through experience, men have learned that if they beat their wives with a stick that is too large, they may end up killing them. Make the stick thin, and the wives should survive. That false tale helped change the overall meaning.

The popular, but incorrect, explanation of the meaning of "rule of thumb" is an example of . . .

A.   folk music
B.   folksy charm
C.   folk etymology
D.   none of the above

(Answer: c)

8TH PERIOD

Engish

Librarian by Day...

Allegory

AN ALLEGORY IS AN ILLUSTRATIVE STORY or parable—a story in which the characters and happenings are meant to represent deeper, more symbolic meanings than their surface meanings would suggest. *Allegory* comes from the Greek word *allegoria*, meaning a "description of one thing under the image of another." That word, in turn, comes from two Greek halves: *allos*, meaning "different" or "something else" (you'll see the same root in the word *alias*), and *agoreuein* meaning "to speak openly."

In ancient Athens, if you wanted to criticize a public official, you sometimes had to use an *allegoria*—or, as we would say, "allegory"—to criticize that official in a roundabout way, without mentioning him by name. You would "speak openly" about "something else"—and make your point indirectly without having to incur any danger or risk. Eventually, the *allegory* became a literary form whose main purpose was to make the hearer or reader think about the connections between what the various elements were supposed to represent.

Famous allegories include Aesop's *Fables* and George Orwell's *Animal Farm*. I'd throw in the film *V for Vendetta*, too. Half the fun in these stories, of course, is figuring out what represents—or conceals—what.

The movie *V for Vendetta* is an allegory for a famous character in English history. Who was that character?

A. James Bond
B. Guy Fawkes
C. Shakespeare
D. Lady Diana

(Answer: b. Fawkes was an English Catholic who attempted to blow up the Houses of Parliament in 1601 to displace Protestant rule.)

Blurb

IN 1907, A WRITER by the name of Gellett Burgess was trying to come up with the copy that would grace the rear cover of his new book, *Are You a Bromide?* Back then, book publishers were a great nuisance, because they would pressure authors, usually at the very last minute, to connect with prominent, hard-to-reach people and persuade them to go on the record with a quote praising the author's book, suggesting that the author deserved to be laminated, or elected president, or both. (Which, of course, is not anything modern-day publishers would dream of doing!)

Burgess seems to have resented the job of begging famous people to come up with nice things to say about him in print, because he refused to do it. Instead, he wrote a parody of the rear-cover endorsements of his era, and invented a fictitious character named Belinda Blurb as a stand-in celebrity. Belinda, an attractive but completely unknown young lady, was dutifully pictured on the back cover praising Burgess's new book. The joke gave rise to a new word within the publishing industry: *blurb*. This means a short expression of written praise about a book, author, or similar work.

I am trying to reach Miss Blurb right now to see whether she will give me a quote. Maybe you will, too. Please visit www.hotforwords.com/blurb, and tell me what you think of this book.

The word *bromide*, which appeared in the title of the book that first used the word blurb, means . . .

- A. a boring old saying
- B. part of a chemical compound
- C. a person who just won't stop talking
- D. all of the above

(Answer: d)

Comma

I ask you my dear student is it possible even to imagine
life without the *comma* that essential all-too-often
overlooked punctuation mark that indicates a pause in a
sentence such as say this one? What for instance would
this sentence look like if there were no comma with which
to you know separate one section of the text from another
and thereby give you the reader a chance to breathe in the
event that you happened to be reading the lengthy text
aloud which is of course always a possibility? Would you
wish even to continue reading the next sentence of such
a comma-deprived entry an entry I should point out that
would be devoted not only to the essential nature of the
punctuation mark itself but also of course to the origin of
the very word we use to describe it?

Enough of that, I think. Look, I have my commas back.
Hooray! I felt naked without them.

The word *comma* also means . . .

A. a species of butterfly
B. a clause in Greek rhetoric
C. an operator used in the programming language C
D. all of the above

(Answer: d)

THE WORD *COMMA* COMES FROM the Greek word *komma*, which simply means "a piece cut off." This is a relatively straightforward derivation, pointing as it does to the nature of an indispensable punctuation mark that separates one portion of a sentence from another.

There's been a big debate for some years about whether a comma should come after each item in a list appearing in a sentence: the first item, the second, the third, and so forth. If you are one of those people who holds stubbornly to the opinion that the comma after the word "third" in the previous sentence should have been omitted, consider the following famously messy book dedication that some editor took it into his head to correct. As the author originally had it, it read: *This book is dedicated to my parents, Emily Dickinson, and God.* After the editor had gotten done "cleaning it up," it read: *To my parents, Emily Dickinson and God.*

Garble

IT MEANS "CONFUSED or corrupted," and it usually refers to the unintentional distortion of a signal or message. The word *garble* comes from the Arabic word *gharbala*, which meant to sift something—spices for instance—and examine the result closely.

Garble was a common trading word for centuries. It eventually came to mean the possibly intentional corruption or adulteration of an original product, and the leap from that to a mixed-up message was a natural one. This usage in English— the sense of a "garbled" message—dates back to the late seventeenth century.

There used to be a *garbler* of spices in the city of London who had the authority to examine spices, drugs, and other products by sifting them. He was a forerunner of the modern Food and Drug Administration in the United States. Back then, to *garble* meant to find impurities and flaws; now it means to introduce them.

A century or so ago, the dictionary said garble meant . . .

A. to pick out such parts as may serve a purpose

B. to imitate Greta Garbo

C. to pretend to consume spice

D. to make a confused sound with liquid in the mouth

(Answer: a)

Glossalgia is . . .

- A. the study of glossy things
- B. nostalgia for glossy things
- C. a pain in the tongue
- D. a brand name of lip gloss

(Answer: c)

Glossary

What part of your body explains something? Yes, yes, your mouth. But what *part* of your mouth? In addition to the lips, I mean.

Right: the tongue.

THE GREEK WORD *GLOSSA* MEANS "tongue." Over a period of centuries, as part of a very slow evolution, *glossa* also came to mean "word," and, eventually, "the explanation of a foreign word." It's not too surprising, then, that the English language would one day settle on the word *glossary* to describe a list of explanations or definitions, such as the one that appears at the end of a textbook.

The same root gives us the English word *gloss*, meaning a brief definition or description. Beware: The other English word *gloss*, the one meaning luster or shine, derives from a completely different source, the Icelandic noun *glossi*, meaning "flame."

Don't confuse the two—and don't go putting your tongue on something that's too hot, either.

Censor

WILL ANYONE EVEN ADMIT to being a censor anymore? I don't think so. They are definitely still around, though.

Today, we think of a censor as a person who removes or obscures material considered too explicit, sensitive, or shocking for general circulation. The word comes from the Latin verb *censeo,* which means "to rate, estimate, or assess." Back in the days of ancient Rome, the *censors* were the officials who took the *census,* that is, conducted a formal count of the population every five years. Not only did these officials produce a tally of the citizenry, they also kept track of the moral lapses they encountered during their surveys—lapses such as sexual immorality and the abuse of slaves. When we say that someone is *censorious,* we are remembering the role of the Roman *censors* as upholders of public virtue and condemners of open vice.

The modern censor's job is different: finding and removing objectionable material from mainstream display or publication in art, literature, media, or journalism—or, in the national security realm, restricting the circulation of potentially damaging intelligence information.

~~Most of this book was originally about how aliens have taken over our government and the subsequent cover-up, but the censors wouldn't allow us to print that.~~

Comedian George Carlin's routine, "Seven Words You Can Never Say on Television," was . . .

A. so heavily censored that it was never released on LP

B. so heavily censored that it was never played on the radio during Carlin's lifetime

C. one of the central disputes at issue in a 1978 U.S. Supreme Court case

D. a letdown, since the supposedly "dirty words" turned out to be Bashful, Doc, Dopey, Grumpy, Happy, Sleepy, and Sneezy

(Answer: c)

Now that you know what an ampersand is, can you tell me what the name of this symbol is?

A. aintpersand
B. squiggly thing
C. heart icon
D. dingbat

(Answer: d)

& (Ampersand)

If you've ever seen the symbol & and wondered what its name was or how it came to be, you're not alone.

THIS SYMBOL IS CALLED an "ampersand." The ampersand dates back to a Roman named Tiro who came up with what would turn out to be a very influential abbreviation around 63 B.C. Tiro had been hired by the great orator Cicero to keep track of, and write out, Cicero's speeches. Not one to waste time, Tiro took the Roman word for *and*—which was *et*—and squished the two letters *e* and *t* into a single character that was easier for him to write:

The abbreviation stuck. You can probably see how that symbol eventually morphed into the one we use today. The name *ampersand* didn't show up until 1837, though, when someone was compiling a list of English-language symbols and wrote down this phrase to explain Tiro's (now ancient) "innovation":

& per se = and

If you read it out loud, you'll say something like "and per se and." The Latin phrase *per se* means "by itself." All the notation really was trying to get across was this: "When you see this symbol—&—by itself, it means 'and.'" The notation was eventually compressed to the word *ampersand*, which now serves as the name of the symbol.

Social Studies

Sex, Lies, and Politics

Candidate

Why are people who run for office called "candidates"— and since when does being a politician have anything to do with being candid? Most of the political candidates I've seen have done a pretty good job of being *less* than candid.

BACK IN THE DAYS OF ANCIENT ROME, the Latin word *candidus* meant "free of bias, clear, sincere, and impartial." Like me, however, you probably wondered *what on earth any of that has to do with politicians.* Well, *candidus*, which came from the verb *candere,* "to shine or glow outwards," also meant "white"—and that gives us our first big clue about the derivation of the word *candidate.*

During the days of the Roman Republic, people who aspired to hold public office would make public appearances, just like today's politicians. When they made those public appearances, they wanted to be sure to leave the best impression possible with the crowds, and in the world of Roman politics, that meant wearing an immaculate white tunic. The cleaner and brighter the white tunic was, the better the job the person running for office was doing at dressing for success. Thus, the Latin word *candidatus* originally meant "someone dressed in white."

Now you know the connection. By the way, the same Latin root—*candidus*—inspired other English words that really did end up having something to do with clarity and light, like *candle* and *incandescent.*

Name the one-time political candidate who was less than clear when he said, "We are ready for any unforeseen event which may or may not happen."

A. Thomas Dewey

B. Dan Quayle

C. George W. Bush

D. Ronald Reagan

(Answer: c)

Caucus

A CAUCUS IS DEFINED as a "gathering of political supporters." In the United States, a *caucus* is either a meeting at which party-affiliated voters directly negotiate the selection of their locality's delegates, as part of the national presidential nominating process, or a gathering of congressional members belonging to a certain group or subgroup. In nations of the British Commonwealth, a caucus is a scheduled, official meeting of one of the parties represented in Parliament.

Just as many people are mystified about what politicians actually do when they're not running for office, a lot of people are mystified about the origin of this word. There seems to be consensus that it came from America, but that's where the agreement ends. The two leading candidates are the Algonquin tribe of Virginia, whose word *caucauasu* meant "counselor," and the liquored-up Caucus Club of Boston, which appears to have taken its name from the Greek word *kaukos*, which was a drinking cup. Both are plausible, since members of the Tammany Hall political machine, which helped to popularize the term, had members who liked to both appropriate Native American terms *and* drink a lot.

Which author parodied British caucus meetings?

A. Lewis Carroll
B. J. R. R. Tolkien
C. Ian Fleming
D. F. Scott Fitzgerald

(Answer: a, Lewis Carroll, in his book *Alice in Wonderland*. The episode "A Caucus-Race and a Long Tale" sends up pointless English political gatherings.)

GOP

Maybe you've run into this abbreviation in newspapers and television broadcasts and assumed from the context that it must have *something* to do with the Republican Party. But what? It doesn't even have an *r*, which is a little weird if it's the party's abbreviation, right?

SOME OF THE THINGS PEOPLE HAVE PROPOSED—not always very seriously—as explanations for the initials GOP are more than a little weird (or just plain partisan). Is this organization a gathering of "Grizzly Old People"? Is it "God's Own Party"? "Gas, Oil, and Petrol"?

No, no, and no; the real story behind *GOP* has less flamboyant origins.

Political parties tend to create their own legends and counter-legends, and the major American parties are no exception. The Republican Party was founded in 1854 by antislavery activists, and it rose to power for the first time in 1860 with the election of Abraham Lincoln. The phrase "Grand Old Party" was used to describe the Republicans in 1876, even though, at that point, the party was less than three decades old, and in fact, far younger than the rival Democratic Party. But the name "Grand Old Party" made the newer party sound like an institution that had been around forever.

Someone—presumably party activists—kept pushing the label, and the term "Grand Old Party" eventually became synonymous with the Republicans. This was eventually shortened to *GOP*.

On the basis of this abbreviation, and its underlying name, some people think that the Republican Party has a longer political lineage than the Democrats, which is just not true. (See the next entry.)

The color scheme of red representing Republicans and blue representing Democrats was standardized in what year?

    A.   1890

    B.   1929

    C.   1945

    D.   2001

(Answer: d. I'll bet you thought it was earlier! It was not, however, and was quite often the opposite colors.)

Under Andrew Jackson, the political party in question began to refer to itself as . . .

A. "Democratization"
B. "The Democracy"
C. "The Republic"
D. "The Democratic-Republican Party"

(Answer: b)

Democratic Party

YOU MIGHT THINK that there have always been two main parties in the United States, the Republicans and the Democrats . . . right? Wrong. There have been lots of major political parties in the United States over the years. The two "big-tent" parties we have today are simply the survivors of a long process of competition and consolidation. But who goes to a Whig rally these days? Or a Progressive Party convention? Or a Know-Nothing assembly? Those parties are long gone, of course, but the names were cool while they lasted.

Some people say there's no real difference between the two dominant parties in the United States today. I don't know whether they are right or wrong about that, but here's an interesting question to consider: How close did we come to having a two-party system that consisted of the Republicans and . . . the Republicans?

The party we today know as the "Democratic Party," which dates back to Thomas Jefferson, originally called themselves the "Republican Party"—much to the confusion of history students who would associate that name with the (much later) political movement that opposed slavery and elected Abraham Lincoln to the presidency in 1860.

Back in Jefferson's day, though, people who opposed his Republican party tried to paint Jefferson and his backers as proponents of mob rule . . . and the general chaos that accompanies it. To do this, they started calling him and his followers "Democratic," and they didn't mean it in a nice way. Believe it or not, the Democrats are only called by that name today because their opponents thought it was a good insult. The insult eventually became the official name of the party.

Gung Ho

If we know anything about the U.S. Marines, we know that they're extremely gung ho. Do we know what *gung ho* is, though?

IT'S A CHINESE PHRASE MEANING "Work in Harmony," and though that may sound vaguely Maoist, the Marines got it from pre-Communist China, during that country's 1937 resistance campaign against the Japanese. Brigadier General Evans F. Carlson was stationed in the mountains of North China so that he could observe Chinese guerrilla action against the Japanese firsthand. He heard the slogan shouted out by Chinese fighters and was impressed by its apparent galvanizing effect on the Chinese troops. He dug a little deeper and found out what it meant.

Later, Calrson was placed in charge of the Second Marine Raider Battalion during World War II. He chose *gung ho* as both the unit's slogan and his personal leadership philosophy. Years later, he explained the Chinese term he had adopted as follows:

"Gung Ho! To Work in Harmony! Our goal: to create and perfect a cohesive, smooth-functioning team, which by virtue of its harmony of action, unity of purpose, and its invincible determination, will be able to out-point the enemy on every count."

In contemporary usage, *gung ho* has come to mean "zealous and extremely energetic."

The 1943 film *Gung Ho*, which popularized the term, was about . . .

A. the Second Raider Battallion's 1942 raid on Makin Island

B. the defeat of pesky Communist insurgents in rural China

C. Japanese espionage networks in California

D. Chinese political instability during the late 1930s

(Answer: a)

Elbridge Gerry, the man after whom the Gerrymander was named, was also famous for . . .

A. refusing to sign the Declaration of Independence when he was asked to

B. refusing to sign the Constitution when he was asked to

C. refusing to sign autographs as "Elbridge 'The Beast' Gerrymander" when he was asked to

D. none of the above

(Answer: b. He was one of three men who refused to sign the Constitution, though asked to do so—because it did not yet have a Bill of Rights.)

Gerrymander

Have you ever seen a real, live gerrymander? Me neither. That's because it's not a real-life animal, but an interesting example of political evolution.

IN THE YEAR 1812, certain members of the Massachusetts political establishment contrived to reshape the electoral map for Essex County to favor their party in the upcoming elections. A political cartoonist noted that the boundaries of the new congressional district vaguely resembled a salamander, and created a memorable cartoon identifying the "beast" that had emerged as a "Gerrymander." This was a combination of "Gerry" (Elbridge Gerry was the governor of Massachusetts at the time, and a powerful political figure) and the back end of the word *salamander*. The new noun *gerrymander* quickly entered the political lexicon, though it is used today almost exclusively as a verb, *to gerrymander,* meaning "to create geographical boundaries that favor one political party over another." *Salamander* dates to the fourteenth century, and appears to have been coined to describe a mythical Greek lizard who could not be killed by fire—now it describes a real lizard. In the 1700s, *salamander* became slang for "a woman who lives chastely despite great temptation." I don't think that's what the Founding Fathers were getting at, though.

Poll

IF YOU VISITED THE United States from another planet during campaign season, you might think that preliminary polls were the most important part of the democratic system, and the act of casting the ballot on election day was only a formality. What's most interesting about polls to me, though, is not their ability to forecast the results of an election, but the many ways the word is used to describe different aspects of the voting process.

We use informal "straw polls" to tell us what the general, but not official, feeling of a group is; we talk about a "polling place," and we mean the location where we cast our votes; we regularly appeal to "pollsters" to tell us who's likely to win the election; and back in the days of segregation, racist politicians tried to exclude minority voters by means of a "poll tax." Stack them all up to see what they have in common: it's the act of "counting heads," which is exactly what the etymology of *poll* points to. The Middle English word was *polle,* which literally meant "the hair on the top of the head." When you counted people who were standing in a crowd, the hair on the top of their heads is what you could, if you were standing up high, expect to see. So that's what you were counting: *polle.*

Once upon a time, the verb *polle* also meant ...

A.   to forecast an election

B.   to cut someone's hair

C.   to hold a pole aloft

D.   to submit a fraudulent voter registration card

(Answer: b)

Radical

DID YOU KNOW that when you call someone a "radical," you are (indirectly) comparing the person to a *radish*?

This is because the ancestor of both *radical* and *radish* is the Latin word *radix,* which means "root." These days, when we call someone a *radical,* we usually mean the person is on the furthest extreme of a party or movement. But the earliest political sense of the word had to do with reformers who were willing to "get to the root" of a social problem. This usage appeared around the beginning of the nineteenth century. Eventually, the word *radical* came to mean what it means today: "Someone who not only believes in a political philosophy I disapprove of, but believes in the most far-fetched elements of that philosophy."

What does any of this have to do with the *radish*? That humble vegetable is, of course, a simple root—which is how it got its name.

I love to ponder such roots.

Who said: "When you are right you cannot be too radical; when you are wrong, you cannot be too conservative."

A. Robert Frost
B. Walt Whitman
C. Martin Luther King, Jr.
D. Mark Twain

(Answer: c)

Besides Uncle Sam, what was the name of the female character who also served as national symbol of the United States?

A. Aunt Bea
B. Columbia
C. Ursula Smith
D. Aunt Samantha

(Answer: b)

Uncle Sam

Was there really an *Uncle Sam*—a living, breathing individual who inspired the bearded, behatted older gentleman who today personifies the United States of America?

AS IT TURNS OUT, no. Uncle Sam was invented around 1813—while the United States was at war with Britain—as a contrast to John Bull, who was the personification of the English nation.

The abbreviation of the United States—U.S.—played a part in the creation of the name Uncle Sam, as that name had the same initials. Over the years, various stories were concocted attempting to attach a real person to the name. Even Congress embraced what seems to be folk etymology in 1961 when it officially adopted a resolution honoring Uncle Sam Wilson of Troy, New York, "as the progenitor of America's National symbol of Uncle Sam." There's a story about him getting the nickname from a bunch of soldiers who really enjoyed his canned meat, but this, of course, was untrue.

So if there's no real Uncle Sam, who is it we see pictures of? The man who painted the iconic image of Uncle Sam in the 1917 World War I poster was named James Montgomery Flagg, and used his own face as a model for the Uncle Sam character— he supposedly didn't want to bother with the details of getting a model.

Tank

No, I don't mean a large compartment for holding water—I mean one of those big armored vehicles that can go almost anywhere. But now that you mention it . . . why do those two things share the same name, anyway?

AS IT HAPPENS, the big armored vehicles were originally known as *landships,* but the British authorities who were entrusted with the task of keeping them secret back in the days of World War I had to come up with something less obvious to use as a name. They called the components used in the machines' construction "tank" components, because that's kind of what they looked like when disassembled—pieces you would use to build a water tank or some other kind of tank. The subterfuge worked for a while, but the name *tank* eventually took over the show. It stopped being a code word and started being the name of the invention itself, making it a bit less useful. (Later code words for tanks included "water tanks" and "turtles.")

In his autobiography, Winston Churchill said the engineering drawings for what would eventually come to be known as "tanks" were originally labeled as . . .

A. water carriers for Russia
B. tanks for the memories
C. water balloons
D. none of the above

(Answer: a)

Advanced
Placement

Tongue Twisters

Floccinaucinihilipilification

Wow. What a strange word! Why is it so long? Where did it come from? What does it mean? Truth in advertising department: I struggled to pronounce this word, but I eventually succeeded. Don't ask me to pronounce the other words in this section, because I won't do it.

THE WORD COMES FROM the eighteenth century *Eton Latin Grammar*, a book published by Eton College in the UK, which helpfully listed for its readers a sequence of Latin words that all equated somehow to the concept of "worthlessness and insignificance."

flocci = trivial

nauci = worthless

nihili = nothing

pili = hair (a single strand of hair was apparently
emblematic, to the Romans, of insignificance)

What happened next? Some schoolboy lined them up, added a suffix, and created what was, for a while, the longest word in the English language—at twenty-nine letters. (It's since been surpassed, arguably, by *pneumonoultramicroscopicsilicovolcaniconiosis*, which describes a type of lung disease. But since that word was coined in 1935 by Everett Smith, then president of the National Puzzler's League, as an example of a really long word, some people don't consider it to be legitimate.)

Of course, you already knew that the word means "the action or habit of judging something to be totally worthless"—didn't you?

People are much too cynical these days. I'll promise not to engage in floccinaucinihilipilification in mixed company if you will, too.

Eton College was founded in . . .

A. 1840
B. 1963
C. 1440
D. 800 B.C.

(Answer: c. The founder was none other than King Henry VI, and recent alumni include Prince William and Prince Henry.)

Antidisestablishmentarianism

THERE ARE A LOT OF CONTENDERS for the title of longest word in the English language. This one has "only" twenty-eight letters—compare *floccinaucinihilipilification*, with twenty-nine, which I just discussed with you. Some people think that *antidisestablishmentarianism* has the advantage, though, because it is neither a "coined" word artificially created just for the purpose of having a very long word (like *floccinaucinihilipilification*), nor a technical word that is of interest only to a narrow group of specialists in some special discipline or other.

Antidisestablishmentarianism is legitimate. It was—and is—a real word that entered mainstream usage to describe a certain political viewpoint, even though it is now used almost exclusively as an example of what a really, really long word looks like, in, you know, books like this.

So—what did it mean originally? Back in 1838, the Church of England saw itself as the "established" (that is, official) church of, well, England. The government saw it that way, too. People who supported this idea of an official state church were called "establishmentarians."

Some people disagreed with the establishmentarians. They felt that the Church of England should not get the special support and patronage it received from the state. What were these people to be called? "Disestablishmentarians," of course, because they wanted to *disestablish* the Church of England.

The supporters of the Church's special position in English society opposed the disestablishmentarians. Now, it's at this point that someone should have probably stepped in and stopped the fight by coming up with a whole new name for the people who specifically opposed the philosophy of *disestablishmentarianism*. What could we have called the people who rejected this position? Anything. Anything except followers of "antidisestablishmentarianism." But that's what someone decided to call them. Their position was that there was no justification for the belief that a nation should be stripped of its official church—plus, the word sounded cool!

Now, what would happen if people opposed those who opposed those who supported the establishment of a state church . . . would they then be called "antiantidisestablismentarians"? OK, maybe this is going too far!

Who was the most prominent figure to use the word *antidisestablishmentarianism* in print—as something other than an example of a really long word?

A. William Gladstone, in his book *Church and State*

B. John Stuart Mill, in his book *On Liberty*

C. Karl Marx, in his book *Das Kapital*

D. James Boswell, in his book *The Life of Samuel Johnson*

(Answer: a)

Honorificabilitudinitatibus

THIS IS A REAL WORD, twenty-seven letters in length, and the single longest word appearing in the works of William Shakespeare. It is also, so far as anyone can figure out, the longest English word in which consonants always alternate with vowels. It means, "the state of being able to achieve honors."

There are lots of interesting theories about why Shakespeare used this word. Some people think it's an elaborate code word that was designed to say something about whether or not the plays of Shakespeare were really written by Shakespeare. The word also shows up in the papers of Sir Francis Bacon, which some people think is evidence that Bacon really wrote Shakespeare's plays.

Honorificabilitudinitatibus also appears in the works of the Elizabethan playwright Thomas Nashe, and James Joyce used it in his novel *Ulysses* in the twentieth century.

If we look at the word, it appears to be a grandiose extension of the Latin word *honorificabilitudo*, which means "honorableness"—from *honorificabilis*, meaning "honorable." Throw a couple of Latin suffixes on the word and voilà!, honorificabilitudinitatibus!

In what play did William Shakespeare use the word *honorificabilitudinitatibus*?

A. *Romeo and Juliet*
B. *Hamlet*
C. *Love's Labour's Lost*
D. *Timon of Athens*

(Answer: c)

Hot for Words/Advanced Placement

159

Detention

You've Been Naughty

TRUE OR FALSE

TRUE OR FALSE

Running stark
naked through
public gatherings
was a popular
craze in the 1940s.

ANSWER False.
Streaking didn't
become popular
until the 1970s.

Stark Naked

THIS PHRASE, sometimes rendered with a hyphen as "stark-naked," dates, in a slightly different form, to the 1500s. It derives from an old German and Middle Dutch word that seems familiar: *start*. In this case, though, *start* doesn't mean "beginning," but rather the "tail" of an animal. The original phrase, then, was *start naked*, and no, it wasn't the first instruction of a game designed for grown-ups. Instead, it described the state of being "naked even to the tail"—that is, completely nude. The word *stark*, without *naked* to keep it company, continued its development along the same lines.

Today, *stark* means "forbidding in bareness or lack of ornament" or "delivered in plain or harsh terms." In other words—the bottom line, without anything at all to conceal it. *Naked* has meant "nude, without clothing" for a very long time indeed, dating back to the Old English word *nacod*, which carried the same meaning.

Booby

One word I've had a few questions about is *boobalicious*. A glance at the word reveals that it consists of two parts: *booby* plus *-licious*. As it turns out, many of my dear students have also requested a discussion of the origin of the word *booby*.

What's going on here? Why all the interest in the word *booby*?

LET'S LOOK AT THE WORD closely. *Booby* has been around since the late 1500s. It appears to have come from the Spanish word *bobo*, meaning "a stupid person," and also from the *booby* bird, which is a very slow and seemingly unintelligent bird. That leads us to the definitions we find in the Oxford English Dictionary (OED): "A dull, stupid person," and "The last boy in the class; the dunce."

That's the earliest sense, but it's not the only one. OED informs us that *booby* is also slang for "a woman's breast." Wait a minute—could *that* be why everyone is asking about this word? No, that can't possibly be it.

As it turns out, this second, later sense of *booby* appears to have come from the word *bubby*, which itself derives from the German word *bubbi*, meaning "teat" or "part of a woman's breast." That usage in English traces as far back as the middle seventeenth century.

So, *booby* can mean "a stupid person," possibly from the Spanish put-down or the dull bird; it can also mean that which men strain for a glimpse of when they see women leaning over water fountains to get a sip of water on a hot summer day. Another mystery solved.

But now the question is: Is TV called the "boob tube" because it makes you stupid, or because of everything you can see on it these days?

Based on what you've just learned, please tell me why a trap would be called a "booby trap."

A. Because the original booby trap was designed by someone who had breasts

B. Because the original booby trap was designed to catch someone who had breasts

C. Because a booby trap is designed to take advantage of foolish people or creatures

D. Because a booby trap is one that is so poorly designed that it is assumed to have been created by a stupid person

(Answer: c)

The U.S. government created a cartoon character named Private Snafu during World War II.

ANSWER True. His voice was very similar to Bugs Bunny . . . in fact it *was* Bugs Bunny's voice! Come to www. hotforwords.com/snafu to watch the videos for yourself and see what I am talking about.

Snafu

As a noun, it has come to mean "a mistake or mishap caused by human error"; as a verb, "to cause delay or confusion by means of incompetence."

SNAFU'S ROOTS GO BACK to World War II, when American soldiers kept their sense of humor about recurrent, or predictable, problems by dismissing them as follows: "Situation Normal—All Fucked Up." Take the first letter of each word, and you've got an acronym . . . and a new addition to the English language.

There are many variations and amplifications of *snafu*, including:

FUMTU—Fucked Up More Than Usual

JANFU—Joint Army/Navy Fuck Up

FUBAR—Fucked Up Beyond All Recognition

TAUFU—Totally and Utterly Fucked Up

SNAFU has been a part of the English lexicon since it was coined during the War; FUBAR was an obscure younger sibling until it started to gain mainstream popularity by means of the Tom Hanks movie *Saving Private Ryan*, which offered an unflinching look at the realities of World War II as lived by servicemen.

Cock

This is certainly one of the very oldest colloquialisms in English for the male reproductive organ, and maybe the oldest, period.

IT IS NOT EXACTLY A COINCIDENCE that the *cock* that crows in the morning has the same name as the attention-getting body part residing inside a pair of male trousers. According to researcher and historian Barbara Walker, the early-rising, early-crowing bird called the "cock" served as a special totem—an object of religious worship—within a special cult of the phallus in ancient Rome.

The Old English word *cocc* literally meant, "someone who struts around proudly." The mental connection between the proud, strutting bird and the haughty, jutting angle of alert male genitalia persisted from Roman times well into the Middle Ages, and it persists to this day—probably because it is wired deeply into the collective human subconscious. The connection between the bird's aggressive demeanor and the man's aroused state plays out across multiple languages.

Closer to home, the familiar word *cocky* originally meant "lecherous," for reasons that seem obvious enough.

TRUE OR FALSE

The first cockpits were pits dug in the ground in ancient China, where cocks bred for battle would fight to the death.

ANSWER True. The word *cockpit* was later applied to the cramped officers quarters on a sailing ship, and eventually to the little place from which pilots control the flight of an airplane.

Blow

LIKE *COCK*, *BLOW* has both sexual and nonsexual meanings. My guess is the nonexplicit ones—"to cause air to pass rapidly through the mouth," or "a hard hit with a weapon or closed hand"—were not the ones that landed you in detention hall.

Some explicit sexual words, like *cock*, have both double meanings and ancient pedigrees. Others, like *blow*, are relative newcomers to the intricate network of double-entendre land mines that spread out across the English language. An ancient Proto-Indo-European root, *bhle-* has connected *blow* and its ancestors to the idea of "making an air current" for centuries, but the sense of "fellate, perform oral sex upon a male" only dates back to 1933. *Blow job* is even younger, with the first attested reference dating to 1961. Both appear to connect to the use of *blow* as a euphemism—or maybe a joke—describing the male orgasm. (It's possible *blow* in this sense connects to the old whaler's expression, "Thar she blows!") What did people used to call this activity, other than the formal-sounding *fellatio*, before *blow* came along? Apparently, "sucking."

The female version of oral sex, *cunnilingus*, has a more simple origin, it simply comes from the Latin *cunnus*, meaning a woman's vagina, and *-lingus* meaning lick.

Blow is also modern slang for cocaine, due to its association with the nose, and was most likely a code word at one point.

TRUE OR FALSE

A bathhouse discovered near Pompeii featured ancient images of women striking a blow for sexual repression—or something—by giving men oral sex.

ANSWER True.

The F-word

THE INFAMOUS "F-WORD." In its most basic form, it means "to copulate," and it has to be one of the most resilient, versatile, and powerful words in the history of the English language. It can be a noun, a verb, an interjection, a transitive verb, an intransitive verb, an adjective, part of an adverb, even an adverb enhancing an adjective! But, like the comedian Rodney Dangerfield, it gets no respect.

You can *hint* at this word by means of an abbreviation or a euphemism, and you can *do* the activity this word describes, under certain conditions, and discreetly—but *saying* it or *printing* it can still get you in big commercial or social trouble.

The Oxford English Dictionary didn't even list the word when it first completed its "F" volume, probably because printing it had been illegal in Britain since 1857. It had been illegal to print it in the United States since 1873; James Joyce's *Ulysses* used the word and was banned in both the UK and the United States. until Joyce won a landmark U.S. court case in 1933 that allowed him to publish the book in the States.

Due to the fact that this word was illegal to print for so long, it remained Forever Under a Cloud of Knowledgelessness, and all kinds of fake stories were created to make up for the lack of information. Some people to this day still believe that *fuck* is an acronym for Fornication Under Consent of the King, as, in order to control population growth in medieval England, couples would need to get the permission of the King in order to have sex. With his permission, they would receive a sign with the initials *FUCK* to hang on their door, indicating that beyond the door, there was Fornication Under Consent of the King going on. This is, of course, untrue, but a funny story nonetheless.

Another common story is that people found guilty of sexual crimes in Old England were forced to wear clothing with the initials *FUCK* indicating their sentence For Unlawful Carnal Knowledge. This story is also untrue and funny.

The true origin of the word appears to derive from Germanic sources that connect it to the Dutch *fokken,* meaning "to strike," and "to have sexual intercourse"; the Norwegian verb *fukka,* "to copulate"; its Swedish cousin *focka,* "to copulate, push, or strike"; and the Swedish *fock,* meaning "penis." With all this striking going on, the word doesn't sound so pleasurable now, does it?

> **TRUE OR FALSE**
>
> It wasn't until 1933 that the word *fuck* appeared in a single general dictionary of the English language.
>
> **ANSWER** False. It wasn't until 1965 that the word appeared in a general dictionary of the English language!

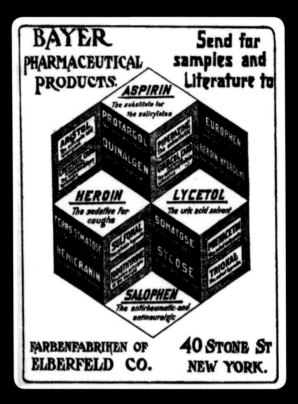

 There was another trademark for a Bayer "miracle drug" that became so popular that the company lost its trademark rights as well. What was it?

a. Aspirin
b. Tylenol
c. Motrin
d. Ibuprofen

(Answer: a)

Heroin

A SERIOUS WORD WITH A SIMPLE EXPLANATION. The reason we call this highly addictive, life-destroying drug *heroin* is that the feeling of power, authority, and control that it (temporarily) imparts makes the person who uses it feel like a *hero* (a man of superhuman strength or courage, from the Greek *heros,* meaning demigod). The *-ine* suffix is applied to many chemicals and substances, like morphine, caffeine, nicotine, etc.

Heroin actually started life as a trademark for a commercial medication in 1898. In the second half of the nineteenth century, there were some very potent "medicines" sold over the counter, and one of these was *Heroin,* a trademarked preparation marketed by Friedrich Bayer & Co. as a "non-addictive morphine substitute" . . . and as a cough syrup for children! Yes, this was really *heroin;* yes, they marketed it as nonaddictive, which was not true; and yes, people gave it to children.

The miracle drug may have soothed the cough, but people eventually caught on that this was not something children should be given by the spoonful. Within a few years, the product was outlawed, and Bayer stopped marketing it. In addition, the term came into such wide use that Bayer lost its trademark rights to the name.

Cocktail

A cocktail is simply a mixed drink, usually one incorporating alcohol. (The secondary meaning, "light appetizer," as in *fruit cocktail,* is a later extension of the word's initial sense of "things mixed together.") The first printed reference to *cocktail* dates back to the early 1800s. The word appears to be American in origin.

SO MUCH FOR THE BASIC FACTS. What you really want to know is this: how did the two halves of this word, *cock* and *tail,* come to intersect at this particular corner of the English language?

The best answer we have is that *cock* and *tail* really didn't come together here at all, except maybe in a hasty (or drunken) piece of mispronunciation. The most plausible explanation for the origin of this word is as follows. Mixed drinks were served by an apothecary named Antoine Amedee Peychaud around 1795 in New Orleans—in an egg cup. (You know—one of those little cups designed to make it easy to eat a boiled egg that's still in its shell.) The French word for "egg cup"—and thus the word Peychaud would have used for the vessel in which he served his drinks—is *coquettier.* English speakers corrupted this to *cocktay,* probably after having downed a few beverages served to them in egg cups. Within a few years, this had evolved, boozily, into *cocktail.*

There are a whole lot of counterexplanations fighting for attention on this one, but Peychaud's egg-cup innovation seems to have the best shot (as it were) at historical accuracy.

Speaking of shots, here's to historical accuracy. Bottoms up!

Alternate explanations of the etymology of cocktail that have been proposed with a straight, or perhaps slightly inebriated, face include . . .

A. Barrel taps were, back in Colonial times, called "cocks"; the dregs of an alcoholic drink were known as "tails." Patrons of taverns would request the "cock tailings" because they enjoyed drinking the dregs.

B. Fighting cocks were forced to drink a swig of liquor before a bout with a fellow rooster, who might or might not have been sloshed. The stuff they gave roosters to drink was called "cock's-ale."

C. People used to enjoy mixed drinks as a morning beverage, and the "cock" part of the word has to do with the fact that people who downed a morning cocktail considered themselves to be announcing a new day, just as a crowing rooster would.

D. People used to put feathers from a cock's tail into alcoholic beverages as decoration.

E. All of these explanations have been put forth as possible etymologies of cocktail.

(Answer: e)

Dope

You may have noticed that the word *dope* carries many different meanings—"illegal narcotics"; "a foolish or stupid person"; "inside information," as in "the straight dope"; or "excellent or superior"—if you follow hip-hop terminology, that is.

No, I don't want to smoke any *dope* (narcotics). That would not be *dope* (excellent) in my world, and would make me a *dope* (foolish person). All I want is the straight *dope* (inside information) on a simple question: How did the word *dope* come to have so many meanings?

AS IT HAPPENS, the word derives from the Dutch word *doop*, which simply means "a thick dipping sauce." By the middle of the nineteenth century, though, the plot had thickened. (Sorry.) At that point, the word *dope* was used to describe the syrupy medicines that doctors gave their patients. Some of those medicines had a stupefying effect. They made you drowsy and caused you to start mumbling and slurring your words, making people think you were stupid—or a "dope."

By the end of the 1800s, the word also started to refer not just to any thick, syrupy preparation, but to opium, which was in a goopy state before being smoked. A headline from a May 1888 *Los Angeles Times* article screamed:

"DOPE" FIENDS:
Police officers raid a Notorious Den
A Sallow-Faced Pipe-Hitter and
a Nude Female captured
A Disgrace to Civilized Los Angeles
The Unforturnate Girl Weeps Bitter Tears

Heavy stuff! Before long, the phrase "dope fiend" had become a household word.

It gets even more interesting. In the world of horse racing, corrupt insiders would sometimes influence the outcomes of races without bettors ever knowing what was going on. How did they do it? By "doping" the horses, of course. If you happened to be one of those insiders who possessed the list of horses who had been doped, you had valuable, accurate, confidential information: the straight dope.

Fast-forward to the 1980s, which was the period when certain rappers started using *dope* as a synonym for *excellent*. This was supposedly a reference to the feeling they experienced while high on heroin. And now *you've* got the straight dope on how *dope* attracted so many meanings!

A dope-shop is ...

A. a place where illegal drugs are sold
B. a store where the employees are foolish or stupid
C. a place where dope is given to horses
D. a place where dope is applied to airplanes

(Answer: d. Dope is also a varnish applied to the cloth surface of airplane parts to increase their strength and keep them airtight.)

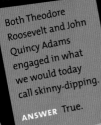

TRUE OR FALSE

Both Theodore Roosevelt and John Quincy Adams engaged in what we would today call skinny-dipping.

ANSWER True.

Skinny-Dipping

I was skinny-dipping the other day, and while I was swimming around, I began to wonder: Why is it called "skinny-dipping," anyway? Here was a mystery!

Yes, we all get the "dipping" part—but what about the "skinny"? And what happens if you are not so skinny? Can you still skinny-dip?

TO SKINNY-DIP MEANS, of course, to swim naked. The "dipping" half of this verb has been used to describe swimming since early Colonial days. We still find it used in phrases like "take a dip in the pool."

The *skinny* part also goes a long way back in time. Though it means "slim" today, it actually used to mean "having to do with skin." That usage dates all the way back to 1573. So: *skinny-dipping* means simply "to swim in one's skin." As in, naked. As in, not wearing any clothes whatsoever. As in, the way I was swimming the other day while I was thinking about word origins. Anyway, the usage of *skinny-dipping* in English was first recorded in the 1950s, though the two halves of the word, as we have seen, go back much further than that.

By the way, *skinny-dipping* used to be the only way people swam in ancient times. Swimsuits are a fairly recent invention.

Alcohol

BACK IN THE DAY, the Egyptian queen Cleopatra used a metallic ore called "powdered antimony" to "darken and lengthen" her eyebrows.

In Arabic, "powdered antimony" was rendered as *al-kohl*. From that we eventually derived the word *alcool* to mean any powdered preparation or extract. Then people started talking about "alcool of wine," meaning an extract of wine, or what we would call brandy. Then (did you ever notice how many different steps these words sometimes have to go through to make sense to us?) the word eventually came to describe *only* the fermented liquid you drink.

So *alcohol* is one of those words that sounds like it's been around forever, but really hasn't. We've only been using it to describe intoxicating beverages since about 1850. It's interesting that the first cited reference of the term *alcoholic*—"one who is addicted to drinking to excess"—shows up shortly thereafter, in 1852. The phenomenon of drinking too much, though, goes back much, much further.

Consumption of alcohol was at some point made illegal in . . .

- A. the United States
- B. Russia and the Soviet Union
- C. Iceland
- D. all of the above

(Answer: d. All these countries eventually repealed prohibition.)

Extra Credit

Do You Want to Be the Teacher's Pet?

NOW IT'S YOUR TURN. You've come to the extra-credit section of this book, which means that instead of me giving you the answers, it's time for you to earn credit by telling me the right answers.

My challenge to you is that you make your best answers right now. Choose your answers from the quizzes below before you do a Google search or any other kind of research, and e-mail them to me at extracredit@hotforwords.com. By the way, I can tell who's cheating. We will see who has the last laugh.

1. Ha-Ha

You probably already know that "ha-ha" is the sound some people make when they laugh. Which of the following definitions is *also* an accurate definition of *ha-ha*?

A. A nickname for a certain extreme state of female sexual arousal

B. A political party that was popular in the Philippines in the 1890s

C. A special kind of fence designed to be invisible until you get very close to it

D. The original title of James Joyce's *Finnegans Wake*

2. Poop Deck

You've heard of the part of a ship called the "poop deck." It's the raised deck in the back (or stern) of old sailing ships. But do you know why it's called the *poop deck*?

I'll give you three possible origins; see if you can pick the correct one.

A. The poop deck is where the toilets were located.

B. Poop comes from the Latin word *puppis*, which means the stern or back of a ship.

C. *Poop deck* comes from the old days of transporting cow manure. The manure needed to be stored above deck and toward the back, so that the smell would blow away from you.

3. Vanilla

You know the word. *Vanilla* is a flavor and it also means something plain, basic.

Do you have any idea which of these three origins is really where the word comes from?

A. *Vanilla* comes from the *vanilla* plant, which gets its name from the Latin word *vaina* where vagina comes from, as the plant looks like a vagina.

B. *Vanilla* comes from the French *pain-vanillé*—which means "white bread" in English. *Vanilla* was only eaten by the poor, so it was an ordinary dessert, eaten by the common man. Chocolate was reserved for the rich.

C. *Vanilla* comes from Latin *vanus*, which means empty, void. And *vanilla* is void of color . . . because it's white.

4. "Hair of the Dog"

"Hair of the dog" is an expression people use to refer to a remedy for a hangover, meaning to have another drink in the morning to help you get over a hangover. Do you have any idea where the expression comes from?

Here are three possible origins; see if you can pick the correct one.

A. As far back as ancient Rome, they believed that hair from a dog, when mixed with a type of plant and virgin olive oil, was a good remedy for hangovers and other ailments. You would make this disgusting mixture and drink it to make yourself feel better. Yecch!

B. "Hair of the dog" is actually short for "Hair of the dog that bit you," and again we go all the way back to ancient Rome where they believed that similar diseases were cured by similar remedies. If a dog with rabies bit you, you would take some of the dog's hair and put it in your wound to help it heal. Again, yecch!

C. "Hair of the dog" is indeed short for "Hair of the dog that bit you," which comes from a scene in Shakespeare where one of the characters says to the other "What how fellow, thou knave, my fellow you have a haire of the dog that bit you last night." The idea was that, in his hungover state, his hair looks like that of a rabid dog.

Are you ready to become your teacher's pet? Are you feeling brave? How much discipline do you have? Let's find out!

Afterword:
School Is Out for Summer

Thank you, my dear student, for studying with me. You get an A+ for the effort!

Class was fun, right? I hope these lessons exposed you to some fun and exciting origins of words that you and I use every single day—and some that we don't. They make for good conversation starters . . . and they should help you impress members of the opposite sex, because, as I always say, "intelligence is sexy," and that little extra knowledge will make you that much sexier!

Every day I get e-mails from my students thanking me for introducing them to the world of word origins. I hope that I have awakened that curiosity in you as well. Perhaps, moving forward, you will hear a word and think, "I wonder what the origin of that word is?"

This book only covered a few of the fun origins, but I can assure you that there are thousands upon thousands of even more interesting origins!

If you find yourself wondering about the origin of a word or phrase in the future, stop by my website, www.hotforwords.com, and ask me to research it for you. While you are there, tell me what you thought of this book. I'd love to hear from you.

I am at your beck and call! (Wait a minute, where did that expression come from? And what the heck is "beck"? Here I go again!)

About the Author

At only twenty-eight years old, Marina Orlova is already arguably one of the most famous philologists of her time. Fantastic, you might say, but what the heck is a philologist? Well, it's someone who studies linguistics and etymology, and in Marina's case, she focuses on word origins.

Marina has two degrees—Teaching of Russian Language and World Literature Specializing in Philology and Teaching of English Language Specializing in Philology from the State University of Nizhni Novgorod Region in the Russian Federation. But she is best known for her extraordinarily successful YouTube channel called "HotForWords," where every day she takes requests for word origins from online students and makes a video explaining the origin in a fun, animated manner. To date, her videos have been seen over 170 million times!

Marina also appears regularly on the Fox show *The O'Reilly Factor*, discussing pertinent word origins. She was voted the "Sexiest Geek of the Year" by Wired.com, and is regularly named one of the "Hottest Women of the Web" by G4 TV. She can be found daily on her website at www.hotforwords.com or on her YouTube channel, www.youtube.com/hotforwords.

Special Thanks

I'd like to thank the entire YouTube team—you opened the doors for me to be able to reach millions of students with my lessons. I'd also like to thank Brandon Yusuf Toropov for his help in the research and editing phases, Gorby for being such a great cohost, and finally, I'd like to thank all of my students on YouTube and HotForWords.com for being the best behaved students a teacher could ever have!

Index